SOME EARLY EMIGRANTS TO AMERICA

Abstracted by
CREGOE D. P. NICHOLSON, F.S.A.

Reprinted from the *Genealogists' Magazine*
Vol. 12—Nos. 1 to 16
Vol. 13—Nos. 1 to 8

also

Early Emigrants To America From Liverpool

Abstracted by
R. SHARPE FRANCE
County Archivist for Lancashire

Reprinted from the *Genealogists' Magazine*
Vol. 12—No. 7

Published in cooperation with the
SOCIETY OF GENEALOGISTS
London, England

The permission of the Standing Joint Committee of the Middlesex County Record Office to reprint these indentures in book form is gratefully acknowledged. Our thanks is also due to the County Archivist, Miss E. D. Mercer, B.A., F.S.A., for her assistance.

Society of Genealogists

Library of Congress Catalog Card No. 65-25164

Reprinted for Clearfield Company Inc. by
Genealogical Publishing Co. Inc.
Baltimore, MD 1989

American Publishers
GENEALOGICAL PUBLISHING CO.
Baltimore, Maryland

Some Early Emigrants to America

Abstracted by CREGOE D. P. NICHOLSON, F.S.A.

In November 1946 Miss J. Cameron, who was at that time Records Clerk to the Middlesex County Council, read a Paper on the Middlesex Quarter Sessions Records before this Society.[1] In the course of her remarks she mentioned that amongst the Records housed in the Middlesex Guildhall, Westminster, there was " a collection of indentures of persons willing to serve in the Plantations in 1683 and 1684, numbering a thousand, coming from various parts of the country, with details of their address and calling, especially in the 1683 returns. They were to go to Maryland, Virginia, Barbados and Jamaica." Strange though it may seem, this announcement appears to have aroused no interest at the time and nothing further was heard of these documents until Air Chief Marshal Sir Christopher Courtney drew the present writer's attention to them.

An inspection of the documents at once showed their importance and as it appeared that the indentures had never been printed an application was made for permission to print abstracts of all of them in the *Genealogists' Magazine*. This was courteously granted and our thanks were expressed to the late Bt.-Colonel W. H. C. Le Hardy, M.C., the Middlesex County Archivist, and to his Staff, for their willing help and assistance.

An examination of the documents, which are kept in two boxes, revealed that although the indentures were at some time numbered from one to one thousand many of them are now missing and an official count made in June 1948 showed that the remaining indentures total only 758. Many of the documents are damaged and portions (especially at the top) are missing. Fortunately, however, some of the particulars are repeated more than once in the document and this usually enables the missing information to be recovered.

There are two or three different forms of printed Indenture with blank spaces which were filled in in ink. For convenience of reference a specimen of each form is here printed and given a reference letter, which will be used in the abstracts to show which form of wording was used. The first form is as follows, and will be referred to as " Form A." The words in italics are the words filled in in ink in the original.

This Indenture made the *22th.* of .....
Between *Elizabeth fflecher Aged 15 years* of the one party, and *Edward Patteson of White Chapel*
on the other party, witnesseth, that the

[1] Printed in Vol. 10, No. 1, The Genealogists' Magazine.

said *Eliz: fflecher* doth thereby covenant, promise, and grant to and with the said *Edward Patterson* his Executors and Assigns, from the day of the date hereof, until *her* first and next arrival *in Pensilvainia* and after, for and during the term of *Seven* years, to serve in such service and imployment, as he the said *Edward Patterson* or his Assigns shall there imploy *her* according to the custom of the Country in the like kind. In consideration whereof the said .... *Patterson* doth hereby covenant and grant to and with the said *Elizabeth fflecher* to pay for *her* passing, and to find and allow *her* meat, drink, apparrel, and lodging, with other necessaries, during the said term, and at the end of the said term to pay unto *her accordinge to the Costom of the Country.*

In Witness whereof the parties above mentioned to these Indentures have enterchangeably set their Hands and Seals the day and year above written.

Sealed and delivered in the presence of	the mark of X Eliz: fflecher
ffrancis Stile Jon. Ingham	Memorand. the sd. Elizabeth fflecher wth. her Unkle John Jackson & Mr. Jesper Rawlins Churchwarden of Aldgate (her ffather & Mother beinge both dead) did Consent to the sd. Eliz: fflechers Serveinge accordinge to the prt. of the sd. Indenture.
John Jackson. Jasper Rawlins.	Abra. Bayly. Ro: Hastings.

LONDON. Printed for Robert Horn, at the South Entrance of the Royal Exchange.

The Memorandum at the foot is, of course, peculiar to this case and does not occur in other indentures. Abra. Bayly and Ro: Hastings were Magistrates, before whom the Indenture had to be signed.

The second form used, which will be referred to as "Form B," is as follows :—

This Indenture : According to the Method, and by the Order and Direction of his Majestie and most Honourable Privy Councel, Printed and Published in the Thirty Fourth Year of his Majesties Reign of England, &c that now is (1682) That all Servants at any time as are Free and willing to be Retained to Serve in His Majesties Plantations in AMERICA, Are to be duely Examined by any of His Majesties Justices of the Peace, and Bound accordingly, and Recorded in the Court of Sessions ; Now Witnesseth, That *Richard Snell* from *City of London Labourer* Aged *Twenty & seaven* Years, Voluntarily Covenanteth, Promiseth and Granteth to and with *Joseph Ball of*

Rederith In the County of Surrey Marriner from the day of date hereof until his first and next Arrival in the *Island of Barbadoes* and after, for and during the Term of ffower Years therein, shall and will as a Faithful Covenant Servant, serve in such Employment as he the said Joseph Ball his Executors, Administrators or Assignes shall there Imploy *Him* to the custom thereof; In Consideration whereof the said Joseph Ball for Himself, his Executors and Assignes doth Covenant, promise, grant and agree to and with the said *Richard Snell* to pay for his Passage in the good Ship the *Hopewell* Captain *Joseph Ball aforesaid* Commander, or in any other Ship thither Bound, by the Order and Directions of the said Joseph Ball and to find and allow him, Meat, Drink, Apparel, Lodging and Washing necessary during the said Term. And in the End thereof, such other Allowances, as to others are Given and Granted in like kind.

In Witness, &c, the sd. pties. to these present Indentures have Interchangeably put there hands & Seals the ffifteenth day of ffebruary Anno que Regni Caroli Secundi Regit Angliae Tricessimo Quinto Anno Domini 1682.

Sealed and Delivered in   Richard Snell
  the Presence of   X
  George Ison.   his Mark.
                        Examined & bound before me, One of his Mats. Justices of the Peace for the County of Middx. the Day & yeare aforesaid.
                        Abra. Bayly.

The third form of wording, "Form C," occurs at No. 319 and is there given in full. "Form D," slightly different from "Form B," occurs at No. 553.

In order to save space it is proposed to print the particulars in a standardised form as follows:—

(*a*) The type of printed Form, i.e. "A" or "B", followed by the serial number on the document. Then will come all the information about the apprentice, Name, Town from which he came, Occupation and Age. This will be followed by the word "Signs" if he signed the Indenture or an "X" if he signed with a Mark.

(*b*) The Name, Address and Occupation of the person to whom the apprentice was bound. This is often the Master of the ship in which he was to sail.

(*c*) The place to which the apprentice was going. The number of years for which he was bound. The name of the ship in which he was to sail and the name of the ship's Master.

(*d*) The date the Indenture was signed. The names of the Witnesses, and the names of the Magistrate or Magistrates. The latter will be within brackets to distinguish them.

Any special notes on individual Indentures will be added. Where information is missing it must be understood that it is missing on the original document. The earlier documents are those most defective.

ABSTRACTS OF THE INDENTURES.

The series starts with No. 3 which has been printed above (Elizabeth fflecher): Nos. 1 and 2 are missing.

(*a*) A.4. Richard Harris ...... X.
(*b*) William Haveland of St. Ka.... Middx. Merchant.
(*c*) Barbados. 4.
(*d*) 21st. Jan. 1682/3. Richard Waring. Humphry Evans. (Tho. Rowe.)

(*a*) A.5. Christopher Graygoose. X.
(*b*) John Wallis of psh. of Sh .. (? Shadwell) Middx. Mariner.
(*c*) Jamaica. 4.
(*d*) 23rd. Jan. .. Tho. Guy. Wm. Cadd. Jo. Boughton. (H. Smyth. Ro. Harding.)

(*a*) B.6. Joseph Marsh. Oxford. 27. X.
(*b*) Joseph Ball. Roddorith, Surry. Marriner.
(*c*) Barbados. 4. Hopewell.
(*d*) 1682. John Earle. Richard Waring. John Shaw. (Abra. Bayly.)

(*a*) A.7. Charles Webb. 22. Signs.
(*b*) Samuel Nash, London. Merchant.
(*c*) Jamaica. 4.
(*d*) 12th. Feb. .... William Peterkin. Jon. Ingham. (Abra. Bayly.)

(*a*) B.8. John Morerie, Lincolnshire. Labourer. 30. X.
(*b*) as No. 6.
(*c*) Barbados. 4. Hopewell. Capt. Joseph Ball.
(*d*) 1st. (?) Feby. 1682. John Williams. Richard Waring. (Abra. Bayly.)

(*a*) B.9. Thomas Holland, a Taylor from Yorkshire and to work at his Trade. 23.
(*b*) Wm. Haveland of St. Katherines near the Towr. of London. Merchant.
(*c*) Barbados. 4. John & Elizabeth. Capt. Jonas Leech.
(*d*) 1st. Feby. 1682. Humphry Evans. John Williams. (Abra. Bayly.)

(*a*) B.10. Robert Reynolds. Hawsston (? Harston) Cambs. 26. X.
(*b*) as No. 6.
(*c*) Barbados. 4. Hopewell. Capt. Joseph Ball.
(*d*) ..... Edmund Puttinam. John Earle. (Abra. Bayly.)

(a) B.11. Richard Snell. (Printed in full above.)

(a) B.12. John Clifford, from Bridwell. 23. X.
(b) as No. 6.
(c) Barbados. 4. Hopewell. Capt. Joseph Ball.
(d) 19th. Feby. 1682. John Earle. Jon. Ingham. (Abra. Bayly.)

(a) B.13. Trustram Hellmore, from near Exeter, co. Devon. Gardener. 21. Signs.
(b) as No. 6.
(c) Barbados. 4. Hopewell. Capt. Joseph Ball.
(d) 17th. Feby. 1682. John Earle. Richard Waring. John Schaw (?) (Abra. Bayly.)

(a) B. 14. Charles Gaint. Cambridge. Labourer. 21. X.
(b) as No. 6.
(c) Barbados. 4. Hopewell. Capt. Joseph Ball.
(d) 15th. Feby. 1682. Thomas Patterson. John Williams. (Abra. Bayly.)

(a) B. 15. Lewis Sergiant. Wales. Labourer. 22. X.
(b) as No. 9.
(c) Barbados. 4. Hopewell. Capt. Joseph Ball.
(d) 5th. Feby. 1682. John Earle. John Williams. (Abra. Bayly.)

(a) B.16. Samuell Price. Shropshire. Labourer. 22. X.
(b) as No. 6.
(c) Barbados. 4. Hopewell. Capt. Joseph Ball.
(d) 19th. Feby. 1682. John Williams. John Cook. John Oakly. (Abra. Bayly.)

(a) B.17. Mary Sandyford. Yorkshire. Spinster. 20. X.
(b) as No. 9.
(c) Barbados. 4. John & Elizabeth. Capt. Jonas Leech.
(d) 3rd. Feby. 1682. Jonas Abell. Steph. Stowe. (Abra. Bayly. Ro: Hastings.)

(a) B.18. John Peachie. Warinington (sic) co. Northampton. 22. X.
(b) as No. 6.
(c) Barbados. 4. Hopewell. Capt. Joseph Ball.
(d) 17th. Feby. 1682. Richard Waring. William Goodbourne. (Abra. Bayly.)

(a) B.19. Charles Serne (?) City of London. Tapster. 21. X.
(b) as No. 6.
(c) Barbados. 4. Hopewell. Capt. Joseph Ball.
(d) 10th. Feby. 1682. John Arle. Tho. Yatman (?). (Abra. Bayly.)

(*a*) B. 20. Richard Crocker. ffarnw..(?) co. Southampton. 18. X.
(*b*) as No. 6.
(*c*) Barbados. 6. Hopewell. Capt. Joseph Ball.
(*d*) 13th. Feby. 168.. John Earle. Richard Waring. (Abra. Bayly. Ro: Hastings.)

(*a*) B.21. John Cooke. Graise (? Grays) in Essex. ffriender st. (?) 18. X.
(*b*) as No. 6.
(*c*) Barbados. 4. (deleted) Hopewell. Capt. Joseph Ball.
(*d*) 10th. Feby. 1682. John Williams. John Cooke. Richard Waring. (Abra. Bayly. Ro: Hastings.)

(*a*) B.22. Marmaduke Ayles. London. Taylor and to exercise the same. 22. Signs.
(*b*) as No. 6.
(*c*) Barbados. 4. Hopewell. Capt. Joseph Ball.
(*d*) 15th. Feby. 1682. John Earle. Thomas Wisom (?). (Abra. Bayly.)

(*a*) B.23. John Bradford. Downe, co. Kent. 21. Signs.
(*b*) as No. 6.
(*c*) Barbados. 4. Hopewell. Capt. Joseph Ball.
(*d*) 17th. Feby. 1682. Thomas Bradford. William Peterkin. (Abra. Bayly.)

(*a*) B.24. Henery Davis. Bridwell. 18. X.
(*b*) as No. 6.
(*c*) Barbados. 4. Hopewell. Capt. Joseph Ball.
(*d*) 13th. Feby. 1682. Jon. Ingham. mark of James Robiton (? Gobiton). (Abra. Bayly. Ro: Hastings.)

(*a*) B.25. Thomas Webster. Yorkshire. Weaver. 21. X.
(*b*) as No. 6.
(*c*) Barbados. 4. Hopewell. Capt. Joseph Ball.
(*d*) 20th. Feby. 1682. James Williams. John Cook. Richard Waring. (Abra. Bayly.)

(*a*) A. 26. Lamboth Despur. 22. X.
(*b*) William Smyth.
(*c*) Jamaica. 4.
(*d*) 27th. January 1682. ffrancis Branson. Jon. Ingham.
    The sd. Lamboth Despur came before me Abra. Bayly Esqr. one of his Masties. Justices of the peace for the County of Middx. & was Examined & he declared himselfe willing to goe to Jamaica & Serve Wm. Smyth four years.
                  Abra. Bayly.

(*a*) B.27. Thomas Barratt from the county of Worcester. Labourer. 21.
(*b*) as No. 6.
(*c*) Barbados. 4. Hopewell. Capt. Joseph Ball.
(*d*) 12th. Feby. 1682. John Williams. John Cook. Richard Waring. (Abra. Bayly.)

(*a*) B. 28. John Prince. Taylor. Menslo (?) in Shropshire, and to work at his trade. 23. Signs " John Prynce ", in a bold hand.
(*b*) Wm. Haveland. (no address but see No. 9.)
(*c*) Barbados. 4. Hopewell. Capt. Joseph Ball.
(*d*) 11th. Feby. 1682. Humphry Evans. John Williams. (Abra. Bayly.)

(*a*) B.29. William Symmer (?), Suffolk. 23. X.
(*b*) Wm. Haveland, Merchant. (see No. 9).
(*c*) Barbados. 4. John & Elizabeth. Capt. Jonas Leech.
(*d*) 2nd. Feby. 1682. Jon. Ingham. (Abra. Bayly.)

(*a*) B.30. William Mayhoe. 23. X.
(*b*) as No. 9.
(*c*) Barbados. 6. Hopewell. Capt. Joseph Ball.
(*d*) 2nd. Feby. 1682. Richard Waring. (Abra. Bayly. Ro: Hastings.)

(*a*) B.31. Gilbird Goring Gent, from the Kingdom of Scotland. 30. Signs, Gilbert Gordone.
(*b*) William Haveland, Merchant.
(*c*) Barbados. 4. Hopewell. Capt. Joseph Ball.
(*d*) 1st. Feby. 1682. John Williams. Humphry Evans. (Abra. Bayly.)

(*a*) B.32. Martin Finch. Ruskington, co. Lincolne. Labor. 28. X.
(*b*) as No. 9.
(*c*) Barbados. 4. Hopewell. Capt. Joseph Ball.
(*d*) 1st. Feby. 168–. Humphry Evans. William Dounton. (Abra. Bayly.)

(*a*) Handwritten form. 33. Charles Webb. 23.
(*b*) Jonas Leach of London. Mariner.
(*c*) Barbados. 4. John & Elizabeth.
(*d*) 25th. January 1682. Edmond Pattinson. Jon. Ingham. (Abra. Bayly.)

(*a*) A.34. Michell Seyre. 21. Signs Micah Seare.
(*b*) Francis Branson.
(*c*) Barbados. 4.
(*d*) 27th. January 1682. William Smith. Jon. Ingham. (Abra. Bayly.)

(*a*) B.35. Jacob Ruffs. Wattford co. Hertford. Coachman & Groom. 22. X.
(*b*) as No. 6.
(*c*) Barbados. 4. Hopewell. Capt. Jos. Ball.
(*d*) 22nd. Feby. 1682. Tristrem Styles. Thomas Waters. (Abra. Bayly.)

(*a*) B.36. Thomas Walters. Naizborough, co. York. Cordwayner. 24. Signs.
(*b*) as No. 6.
(*c*) Barbados. 4. Hopewell. Capt. Joseph Ball.
(*d*) 22nd. Feby. 1682. Tristrem Styles. Mungo Grant. (Abra. Bayly.)

(*a*) B.37. Thomas Barlow. co. Salop. Ostler & Groom. 21. X.
(*b*) as No. 6.
(*c*) Barbados. 4. Hopewell. Capt. Joseph Ball.
(*d*) 27th. Feby. 1682. John Cooker. John Williams. James Williams. Richard Waring. (Abra. Bayly.)

(*a*) B.38. Rich. Jackson. Bridwell. 31. X.
(*b*) as No. 6.
(*c*) Barbados. 4. Hopewell. Capt. Jos. Ball.
(*d*) Jon. Ingham. John Earle. (Abra. Bayly.)

(*a*) B.39. John Hawkins. co. Wilts. Clothworker. 26. Signs.
(*b*) as No. 6.
(*c*) Barbados. 4. Hopewell. Capt. Joseph Ball.
(*d*) 1st. March 1682. John Cooke. Joseph Pyecraft. (Abra. Bayly.)

(*a*) B.40. John Fairbank. co. Yorke. Yeoman. 31. X.
(*b*) as No. 6.
(*c*) Barbados. 4. Hopewell. Capt. Joseph Ball.
(*d*) 2nd. March 1682. James Howard. Wm. Bond. (Abra. Bayly.)

(*a*) B.41. John Croft. co. Lancaster. Labourer. 21. Signs.
(*b*) as No. 6.
(*c*) Barbados. 4. Hopewell. Capt. Joseph Ball.
(*d*) 3rd. March 1682. John Cooke. William Goodbourn. (Abra. Bayly.)

(*a*) B.42. Thomas Harrison. City of London. Ostler & Groom. 21. X.
(*b*) as No. 6.
(*c*) Barbados. 4. Hopewell. Capt. Joseph Ball.
(*d*) 3rd. March 1682. John Sh . . . (?) John Gillies. (Abra. Bayly.)

(*a*) B.43. James Habbergam. Bridwell. 22. X.
(*b*) as No. 6.

(*c*) Barbados. 4. Hopewell. Capt. Joseph Ball.
(*d*) 26th. Feby. 1683. Jon. Ingham. John Earle. (Abra. Bayly.)

(*a*) B.44. Nathaniell Powell from ye Countie of Lancaster. Woollcomber. 22. X.
(*b*) as No. 6.
(*c*) Barbados. 4. Hopewell. Capt. Joseph Ball.
(*d*) 3rd. March 1682. Joseph Pycraft. Aldred Parris. (Abra. Bayly.)

(*a*) B.45. Jacob Symmons. Oxford. Coachman. 28. X.
(*b*) as No. 6.
(*c*) Barbados. 4. Hopewell. Capt. Joseph Ball.
(*d*) 24th. Feby. 1682. Tho. Puttman. John Sibley. John Earle. (Abra. Bayly.)

(*a*) B.46. Edmond Bullock from the County of Kent. Coachman. 29. Signs.
(*b*) as No. 6.
(*c*) Barbados. 4. Hopewell. Capt. Joseph Ball.
(*d*) 24th. Feby. 1682. James Howard. Richd. Constable. William Anthony. (Abra. Bayly.)

(*a*) B.47. Thomas Bramly. Retten (?Repton) co. Derby. Labourer. 29. X.
(*b*) as No. 6.
(*c*) Barbados. 4. Hopewell. Capt. Joseph Ball.
(*d*) 21st. Feby. 1682. Tho. Puttman. Joseph Pycraft. John Earle. (Abra. Bayly.)

(*a*) A.48. William Wilsheire. Aged 40 years. X.
(*b*) Francis Richardson.
(*c*) New York or New Garsey. 4.
(*d*) 21st. Feby. 1682/3. Jon. Ingham. Israell Morley. (Abra. Bayly.)

(*a*) B.49. John Laymard, from France. 30. X.
(*b*) as No. 6.
(*c*) Barbados. 4. Hopewell. Capt. Joseph Ball.
(*d*) 26th. Feby. 1682. Samuell Smith. James Lambart. (Abra. Bayly.)

(*a*) B.50. George King. Cr . . maker, Bristol City, and to work at ye same trade. 26. Signs.
(*b*) as No. 6.
(*c*) Barbados. 4. Hopewell. Capt. Joseph Ball.
(*d*) 28th. Feby. 1682. John Cook. John Williams. James Williams. Richard Waring. (Abra. Bayly.)

(*a*) A.51. Rich. Browne. aged 33 years.
(*b*) Frances Richardson.

(*c*) New York or New Jersey. 4.
(*d*) 21st. Febry. 1682/3. Israell Morley. Jon. Ingham. (Abra. Bayly.)

(*a*) B.52. Robert Bettally. West Chester. Coachman to follow ye same. 22. X.
(*b*) as No. 6.
(*c*) Barbados. 4. Hopewell. Capt. Joseph Ball.
(*d*) 20th. (?) Feby. 1682. John Earle. Wm. Goodbourne. (Abra. Bayly.)

(*a*) B.53. John Rogers. Bridwell. 18. Signs.
(*b*) as No. 6.
(*c*) Barbados. 4. Hopewell. Capt. Joseph Ball.
(*d*) 16th. Feby. 1682. Jon. Ingham. Tho. Guy. (Abra. Bayly. Ro. Hastings.)

(*a*) B.54. John Benerley. Bridwell. 18. X.
(*b*) as No. 6.
(*c*) Barbados. 4. Hopewell. Capt. Joseph Ball.
(*d*) 16th. Feby. 1682. Jon. Ingham. Tho. Guy. (Abra. Bayly. Ro. Hastings.)

(*a*) B.55. Abell Steere, from the County of Kent. Labourer. 20. Signs.
(*b*) as No. 6.
(*c*) Barbados. 6. Hopewell. Capt. Joseph Ball.
(*d*) 26th. Feby. 1682. John Gillies. Mungo Grant. Aldred Parris. (Abra. Bayly. Ro. Hastings.)

(*a*) B.56. Godfery Beard. Taylor, from the County of Derby, to work at his Trade. 22. Signs Godfrey Beard.
(*b*) as No. 6.
(*c*) Barbados. 4. Hopewell. Capt. Joseph Ball.
(*d*) 3rd March 1682. Tho. Puttman. John Williams. (Abra. Bayly.)

(*a*) B.57. Thomas Barratt from the County of Essex. Butcher. 25. X.
(*b*) as No. 6.
(*c*) Barbados. 4. Hopewell. Capt. Joseph Ball.
(*d*) 23rd. Feby. 1682. John Earle. Tho. Shroud. (Abra. Bayly).

(*a*) B.58. Thomas Smith from Ireland. 22. X.
(*b*) William Haveland of St. Katherines near the Tower of London. Merchant.
(*c*) Barbados. 4.
(*d*) 29th. January 1682. Tho. Puttman. Humphry Evans. (Abra. Bayly.)

(a) B.59. Joel Jones a Taylor from Shropshire and to work at his Trade. 23. X.
(b) as No. 58.
(c) Barbados. 4. John & Elizabeth. Capt. Joseph Ball.
(d) 1st. February 1682. Humphry Evans. John Williams. (Abra. Bayly.)

(a) A.60. John Tyler. Bricklayer. X.
(b) as No. 58.
(c) Plantation of Barbados. 4.
(d) 15th. January 1682. (no witnesses) (Tho. Cheek.)

(a) A.61. John Wetton. Signs John Wettin. Armorial seal.
(b) Robert Lessells of the parish of Stepney in the county of Middlesex. Marriner.
(c) Jemaicoe. 4.
(d) 1st. March 1682. Thomas Tyere. J. Boughton. (W. Smyth. ?)

(a) A.62. Henry Blake. Smith. X.
(b) as No. 58.
(c) Barbados.
(d) 15th January 1682. (no witnesses) (Tho. Cheek.) Lieutenant of the Tower.

(a) A.63. Richard Hepart. Ostler. X.
(b) Thomas Ward of Jamaica, Planter.
(c) Jamaica. 4.
(d) 2nd. March 1682/3. Robert Smith. Geo. Lawson. (Thomas Smith.)

Nos. 64 and 65 missing.

(a) B.66. John Tubb. Wantage in the County of Berks. 25. X.
(b) as No. 6.
(c) Barbados. 4. Hopewell. Capt. Joseph Ball.
(d) 7th. March 1682. Richard Waring. John Shaw. John Williams. (Abra. Bayly.)

(a) B.67. Aaron Leek. St. Ives in ye County of Huntington. 21. Signs Aaron Lake.
(b) as No. 6.
(c) Barbados. 4. Hopewell. Capt. Joseph Ball.
(d) 8th. March 1682. Jon. Ingham. John Earle. (Abra. Bayly.)

(a) B.68. Nicholas Leatherington from Yorkshire. 21. X.
(b) as No. 6.
(c) Barbados. 4. Hopewell. Capt. Joseph Ball.
(d) 6th. March 1682. John Earle. John Buttewisk. (Abra. Bayly.)

(a) A.69. Tho: Sharp. 26. Signs.
(b) John White of Ratcliff.

(c) Barbados. 4.
(d) 7th. March 1682/3. Jon. Ingham. John Buttewisk. (Abra. Bayly.)

(a) B.70. John Edwards. The County of Devon. 23. Signs.
(b) as No. 6.
(c) Barbados. 4. Hopewell. Capt. Joseph Ball.
(d) 10th. March 1682. Tho: Pattman. William Goodbourne. (Abra. Bayly.)

(a) B.71. Robert Borrodon. County of Lincoln. Coachman. 21. X.
(b) as No. 6.
(c) Barbados. 4. Hopewell. Capt. Joseph Ball.
(d) 12th. March 1682. Tho: Pattman. John Shaw. (Abra. Bayly.)

(a) A.72. Jone Diggerey. 22. X.
(b) Francis Blacke.
(c) Barbados. 4.
(d) 13th. March 1682. Jon. Ingham. John Buttewisk. (Abra. Bayly.)

Nos. 73 to 201 missing.

(a) A.202. Ursilla Pepper. 17. X.
(b) Rich. Bills of St. Mary Magdalen, Bermondsey, Southwark. Marriner.
(c) Jamaica. 4.
(d) 18th. July 1683. J. Boughton (?). Bryan Wawen (?). (H. Smyth. Wm. Freeman.)

Nos. 203 to 268 missing.

(a) B.269. Robert Boyer. County of Berks. Sawyer. 25. X.
(b) William Johnson of London, Marriner.
(c) Mariland. 4. Content. Capt. William Johnson.
(d) 3rd. August 1683. Jon. Ingham. (Abra. Bayly.)

(a) B.270. Hugh Owin from London. 21. X.
(b) Walter Hatch of London. Merchant.
(c) Mariland. 4. Mary. Capt. John Harris.
(d) 4th. September 1683. Jon. Ingham. (Abra. Bayly.)

(a) B.271. George Abie (? Obie) from London. Gardener. 24. X.
(b) Walter Hatch of London. Merchant.
(c) Mariland. 4. Mary. Capt. John Harris.
(d) 4th. September 1683. John Earle. Jon. Ingham. (Abra. Bayly.)

(a) B.272. Lawrance Claye from London. 21. Signs.
(b) Joseph Doyne of London. Merchant.

(c) Mariland. 5. Mary. Capt. John Harris.
(d) 4th. September 1683. Jon. Ingham. (Abra. Bayly.)

(a) A.273. Rebecca Bignall. 29. Of St. Giles the fields. X.
(b) Joseph Doyne.
(c) Virginia. 4.
(d) 5th. September 1683. Jon. Ingham. (Abra. Bayly.)

(a) A.274. Grace Shepard of White Chapell. 21. X.
(b) Edward Brook.
(c) Jamaica. 4.
(d) 5th. September 1683. Jon. Ingham. (Abra. Bayly.)

(a) B.275. Samuel Richardson from Banbery in Oxfordshire. Pinmaker. 21. Signs.
(b) Richard Murphy of London. Merchant.
(c) Mariland. 4. Cont(ent). Capt. Wm. Johnson.
(d) 6th. September 1683. Jon. Ingham. (Abra. Bayly.)

(a) A.276. Margerett Rogers. 19. X.
(b) John Wilson.
(c) Merryland. 4.
(d) 6th. September 1683. Jon. Ingham. (Abra. Bayly. Ro. Hastings.)

(a) B.277. Elizabeth Mason from London. Spinster. 21. X.
(b) Wm. Johnson of London. Merchant.
(c) Mariland. 4. Content. Capt. Wm. Johnson.
(d) 6th. September 1683. Jon. Ingham. (Abra. Bayly.)

(a) A.278. Margarett Mastys. 27. X.
(b) Richard Batts of London. Merchant.
(c) Mary Land. 4.
(d) 6th. September 1683. Jon. Ingham. John Bromhead. (Abra. Bayly.)

(a) B.279. John Holmes. County of York. 21. X.
(b) Richard Murphy of London. Merchant.
(c) Mariland. 4. Content. Capt. William Johnson.
(d) 6th. September 1683. Jon. Ingham. (Abra. Bayly.)

(a) B.280. George Everygen. The County of Dorset. 61. X.
(b) Richard Murphy of London. Merchant.
(c) Mariland. 7.
(d) 6th. September 1683. Jon. Ingham. (Abra. Bayly. Ro. Hastings.)

(a) B.281. James Gooding from London. 21. X.
(b) John Lee of London. Merchant.
(c) Mariland. 4. Hanna. Capt. Guester.
(d) 7th. September 1683. Jon. Ingham. (Abra. Bayly.)

(*a*) B.282. John Dowson from London. 18. X.
(*b*) John Lee of London. Merchant.
(*c*) Mariland. 7. Hanna. Capt. Guester.
(*d*) 7th. September 1683. Jon. Ingham. (Abra. Bayly. Ro. Hastings.)

(*a*) A.283. George Adamson. 18. X.
(*b*) John Wilson.
(*c*) Meryland. 6.
(*d*) 7th. September 1683. Jon. Ingham. (Abra. Bayly. Ro. Hastings.)

(*a*) B.284. Rebecka Dorson. Chatham in the county of Kent. Spinster. 16. X.
(*b*) Wm. Haveland of London. Merchant.
(*c*) Mariland. 5. Mary. Capt. John Harris.
(*d*) 7th. September 1683. Jon. Ingham. (Abra. Bayly. Ro. Hastings.)

(*a*) A.285. Thomas Peters fenix Lightwich. 24. X.
(*b*) Rich. Batts.
(*c*) Merryland. 4.
(*d*) 7th. September 1683. Jon. Ingham. (Abra. Bayly.)

(*a*) A.286. Tho. Owines. 28. Signs.
(*b*) James Phillips.
(*c*) Virginia. 4.
(*d*) 7th. September 1683. Jon. Ingham. (Abra. Bayly.)

No. 287 missing.

(*a*) A.288. Howell Jones. 21. Signs (in an educated hand).
(*b*) John Woosley.
(*c*) Jamaica. 4.
(*d*) 10th. September 1683. Jon. Ingham. (Abra. Bayly.)

(*a*) A.289. Henry Surey. 25. Signs Henry Sury.
(*b*) Samuel Phillips.
(*c*) Merryland. 4.
(*d*) 11th. September 1683. Jon. Ingham. (Abra. Bayly.)

(*a*) A.290. Jeane Lewis. 22. X.
(*b*) John Jackson.
(*c*) Virginia. 4.
(*d*) 11th. September 1683. Johes. Ingham. John Earle. (Abra. Bayly.)

(*a*) A.291. Tho. Nason. 21. Signs.
(*b*) John Wilson.
(*c*) Merryland. 4.
(*d*) 11th. September, 1683. Jon. Ingham. (Abra. Bayly.)

(*a*) B.292. Samuell Northerow (? Northorne) County of Leicester. 25. X.
(*b*) James Connaway of London, Marriner & Commander.
(*c*) Mariland. 4. Baltimor. Capt. James Connaway.
(*d*) 11th. September 1683. Jon. Ingham. (Abra. Bayly.)

(*a*) B.293. Martha Reader. Hertfordshire. Spinster. 19. Signs.
(*b*) James Connaway of London. Marriner & Commander.
(*c*) Mariland. 6. Boltymore. Capt. James Connaway.
(*d*) 12th. September 1683. Jon. Ingham. (Abra. Bayly. Ro. Hastings.)

(*a*) B.294. John Harwood from London. 22. X.
(*b*) James Connaway of London. Marriner & Commander.
(*c*) Mariland. 4. Boltimore. Capt. James Connaway.
(*d*) 14th September 1683. Jon. Ingham. (Abra. Bayly.)

(*a*) B.295. Thomas Nightsmith from London. 21. Signs Thomas Knismth.
(*b*) James Conaway of London. Marriner & Commander.
(*c*) Mariland. 4. Boltimore. Capt. James Conaway.
(*d*) 15th. September 1683. Jon. Ingham. (Abra. Bayly.)

(*a*) A.296. Mary Peirson. 21. X.
(*b*) Rich. Lucey.
(*c*) Merryland. 4.
(*d*) 15th. September 1683. Jon. Ingham. (Abra. Bayly.)

(*a*) B.297. John Mitchell from London. 26. X.
(*b*) Christopher Evilling of London. Marriner & Commander.
(*c*) Virginia. 4. William & Thomas. Capt. Xpher. Evilling.
(*d*) 17th. September 1683. Jon. Ingham. (Abra. Bayly.)

(*a*) B.298. John Smith from London. 21. X.
(*b*) James Conaway of London. Marriner & Commander.
(*c*) Mariland. 4. Boltimore. Capt. James. Conaway.
(*d*) 18th. September 1683. Jon. Ingham. (Abra. Bayly.)

(*a*) B.299. Zackeriah Smale from London. Sayer. 21. X.
(*b*) Thomas Wyche of London. Merchant.
(*c*) Land of Caralaina. 4. Recoverie. Capt. Thomas Hasteed.
(*d*) 20th. September 1683. Jon. Ingham. (Abra. Bayly.)

(*a*) A.300. Everilday Prichard. 21. Signs. (A woman.)
(*b*) Samuel White.
(*c*) Virginia. 4.
(*d*) 21st. September 1683. Jon. Ingham. (Abra. Bayly.)

(*a*) A.301. Ann Brown. 22. X.
(*b*) John Thorne.

(*c*) Virginia. 4.
(*d*) 21st. September 1683. Jon. Ingham. (Abra. Bayly.)

(*a*) B.302. Richard Hinde. County of Kent. Baskettmaker. 24. Signs Richard Hind.
(*b*) Thomas Wyche of London. Merchant.
(*c*) Virginia. 4. Recoverie. Capt. Thomas Hasteed.
(*d*) 22nd. September 1683. Richard Waring. William Goodbourne. (Abra. Bayly.)

(*a*) B.303. Mary Chiswell from London. Spinster. 24. X.
(*b*) Thomas Wyche of London. Merchant.
(*c*) Virginia. 4. Endeavour. Captain Thomas Hasteed.
(*d*) 22nd. September 1683. Jon. Ingham. (Abra. Bayly.)

(*a*) B.304. Joseph Marshall of London. 22. X.
(*b*) Nicholas Prin of London. Marriner.
(*c*) Virginia. 4. Richd. & Elizabeth. Captain Nicholas Prin.
(*d*) 22nd. September 1683. Jon. Ingham. (Abra. Bayly.)

(*a*) A.305. Sarah Green. 22. X.
(*b*) John Bancks.
(*c*) Virginia. 4.
(*d*) 24th. September 1683. Jon. Ingham. (Abra. Bayly.)

(*a*) A.306. Abigall Taylor. 24. Signs.
(*b*) Nath. Snow.
(*c*) Barbadoes. 4.
(*d*) 24th. September 1683. Jon. Ingham. (Abra. Bayly.)

(*a*) A.307. Mary Harris. 25. X.
(*b*) James Congden.
(*c*) Virginia. 4.
(*d*) 24th. September 1683. Jon. Ingham. (Abra. Bayly.

(*a*) A.308. Tho. Sison. 21. Signs Thomas Sisson.
(*b*) Nich. Pryn.
(*c*) Virginia. 4.
(*d*) 24th. September 1683. Jon. Ingham. (Abra. Bayly.)

(*a*) A.309. Mary Wrinch. 27. X.
(*b*) Nich. Pryn.
(*c*) Merryland. 4.
(*d*) 24th. September 1683. Jon. Ingham. (Abra. Bayly.)

(*a*) B.310. John Bennett from London. 21. X.
(*b*) Thomas Wyche of London. Merchant.
(*c*) Virginia. 4. Recoverie. Captain Thomas Hasteed.
(*d*) 24th September 1683. John Bromhead. (Abra. Bayly.)

(*a*) A.311. Martha Kimber. 22. X.
(*b*) Nicholas Pryn.

(*c*) Virginia. 4.
(*d*) 24th. September 1683. Jon. Ingham. (Abra. Bayly.)

(*a*) A.312. ffrances Goreham. 24. X.
(*b*) James Congden.
(*c*) Virginia. 4.
(*d*) 24th. September 1683. Jon. Ingham. (Abra. Bayly.)

(*a*) B.313. John Williamson from London. Accomptant. 21. X.
(*b*) Nicholas Pryn of London. Marriner.
(*c*) Virginia. 4. Richd. & Elizabeth. Captain Nicholas Pryn.
(*d*) 24th. September 1683. Jon. Ingham. (Abra. Bayly.)

(*a*) A.314. Symon Pooke. 24. Signs Simon Pooke.
(*b*) Nich. Pryn.
(*c*) Virginia. 4.
(*d*) 25th. September 1683. Jon. Ingham. (Abra. Bayly.)

(*a*) A.315. Eliz. Harvey. 21.
(*b*) John Edwards of South (? Rootes) in Mary Land. Merchant.
(*c*) Maryland. 5.
(*d*) 28th. July 1683. Hellena Blaymy. Jo. Boughton. Samuell Jennings. (Abra. Bayly.)

(*a*) A.316. Dorothy Guttherick (Gutterick in other places) 30 (? 20). Signs Dorothy Goodrick.
(*b*) Charles Parles.
(*c*) Mary Land. 4.
(*d*) 30th. July 1683. Jo. Boughton. John Bromhead. (W. Smyth.)

No. 317 missing.

(*a*) A.318. Anthony Hambleton. X.
(*b*) Michaell Purifoy of Lyme. . . . Middx. Marriner.
(*c*) Virginia. 7.
(*d*) 3rd. .... Jo. Boughton. Ro Tompson. (W. Smyth. Abra. Bayly.)

We now come to the first example of the third form of printed Indenture, which will be referred to as "Form C". The wording is here given in full. The words in italics are the words filled in in ink in the original.

This Indenture made the *Seaventh day of Sept. 1683*: in the *thirty first year of king Charles the second* &c. Between *Elizabeth Jackson Aged 17* of the one Party, and *Arnatt Keckerbart* on the other Party, witnesseth, that the said *Elizabeth Jackson* doth hereby covenant, promise, and grant to, and with the said *Arnatt Keckerbart*: his Executors and Assignes, from the day of the date hereof, untill *her* first and next arrival *in Virginia* and after, for and during the term of *four* years, to serve in such service and imployment as *he* the said *Arnatt Keckerbart* or his Assignes shall there imploy *her* according to the Custome of the Countrey in the like kind. In consideration whereof, the said *Arnatt Keckerbart* doth hereby covenant and grant to, and with the said *Elizabeth Jackson* to pay for *her* passing, and to find and allow *her* meat, drink, apparel, and lodging, with other necessaries during the said term, and at the end of the said term to pay unto *her according to ye Custom of the Country.*

In witnesse whereof the Parties above mentioned, to these Indentures have interchangably set their Hands and Seales the day and year above written.

Sealed and delivered in
the presence of
Edward Brown.
Peter Debous.

the mark of
X
Elizabeth Jackson.

Examined by us two of his majesties Justices of the peace for ye County of Middx.
Cha. Osborne.
Ro: Hastings.

319.

(a) C. 320. Mary Weaver. 23. X.
(b) John Becker.
(c) Virginia. 4.
(d) 17th. September 1683. Edward Browne. the mark of Lettis X Allin. (Cha. Osborne.)

(a) B.321. Roger Croswell. London. 32. X.
(b) Nicholas Prin of London, Mariner.
(c) Mariland. 4. Richard & Elizabeth. Capt. Nicholas Prin.
(d) 19th. September 1683. Edward Browne. John Earle. (Chas. Osborne.) £10 with him.

(a) A.322. Mary Freeman of London. Spinster. 22 or thereabouts. X.
(b) James Galwith of London, Silkthrower.
(c) Maryland in Virginia. 5.
(d) 20th. September 1683. Of. Reynolds. Fran. Booker. (?) (Tho. Cheek.)

(a) A.323. John Malin. Gardiner. X. The mark of John Malin junior.
(b) James Galwith of London. Merchant.
(c) Maryland in Virginia. 4¾.
(d) 1st. October 1683. X the mark of John Malin Senior. (Tho. Check)

    Mdm. that ye day & yeare above written ye above bounden John Malin together with John Malin his father came before me and ye sd. John Malin ye sonn appearing upon examination to be of the age of 18 yeares did both testify &c. &c.

(a) A.324. Susanna Beatson. 19. X.
(b) Thomas Carey of Ratcleiff in ye county of Middx. Marr.
(c) Virginia. 5.
(d) 18th. October 1683. J. Boughton. Tho: Guy. (W. Smyth. Ro: Hastings.)

(a) A.325. Henry Sutheth. 15. X.
(b) John Galwith of Merryland. Planter.
(c) Merryland. 7.
(d) 4th September 1683. James Galwith. Adam Turnbull. (Thomas Smith. Pe: Selfs. ?)

(a) A.326. Phillipp Ryall. 21. Signs Phillip Ryan.
(b) John Galwith of Merryland. Planter.
(c) Merryland. 5.
(d) 4th. September 1683. James Galwith. Adam Turnbull. (Thomas Smith.)

(a) A.327. Thomas Greene. Blacksmith. 30. Signs.
(b) William Fles of King streete in the hamlet of Wapping, in ye parish of Stepney. Marriner.
(c) Jamaica. 4.
(d) 26th. September 1683. Adam Turnbull. Charles Bruice. Geo. Lawson. (Thomas Smith.)

(a) B.328. Rich. Elkins from Dorsetshere. 22. Signs Richard Elkins.
(b) Nicholas Prin of London. Marriner.
(c) Virginia. 4. Richd. & Elizabeth. Capt. Nicholas Prin.
(d) 4th. September 1683. Jon. Ingham. (Abra. Bayly.)

(a) B.329. John Start from London. 16. X.
(b) James Conaway of London. Marriner & Commander.
(c) Mariland. 8. Baltimore. Capt. James Conaway.
(d) 15th. September 1683. Jon. Ingham. (Abra. Bayly. Cha. Osborne.)

(a) B.330. Frances Francklin from Batersey. 20. X.
(b) James Conaway of London. Marriner & Commander.
(c) Mariland. 4. Boltymore. Capt. James Conaway.
(d) 17th September 1683. Jon. Ingham. (Abra. Bayly. Ro: Hastings.)

(a) B.331. John Hannam from London. 20. Signs.
(b) James Conaway of London. Marriner & Commander.
(c) Mariland. 4. Boltymore. Capt. James Conaway.
(d) 18th. September 1683. Of. Reynolds. (Tho: Cheek. Abra. Bayly.)

Nos. 332 to 336 missing.

(a) A.337. Edward Taylor. 24. X.
(b) Tho: Green.
(c) Jamaica. 4.
(d) 27th September 1683. Jon. Ingham. (Abra. Bayly.)

(a) B. (Number torn off.) John Gillmore. County of Middx. 21.
(b) John Clarke of London. Merchant.
(c) Mariland. 4. Duke of Yorke. Capt. John Purvis.
(d) 16th. October (? 1683) Jon. Ingham. (Remainder torn away.)

Nos. to 341 missing.

(a) A.342. Isaac Shafeild. 18. X.
(b) Nicholas Pryn.
(c) Virginia. 4.
(d) 28th. September 1683. Jon. Ingham. (Abra. Bayly. Ro: Hastings.)

Nos. 343 to 350 missing.

(a) A.351. Wm. Pingler (?). 21. X.
(b) Wm. Phillips.
(c) Virginia. 4.
(d) 10th. (?) October 1683. Jon. Ingham (Abra. Bayly.)

Nos. 352 to 354 missing.

(a) B.355. Stephen Hargoose from London. Groome. 23. X.
(b) Thomas Carey of London. Marriner & Master.
(c) Mariland. 4.
(d) 19th. (?) October 1683. John Earle. John Person. (Abra. Bayly.)

Nos. 356 to 363 missing.

(a) B.364. Richd. Stafford from co. Middx. 23. X.
(b) William Haveland of London. Merchant.
(c) Virginia. 4. Duke of Yorke. Capt. John Purvis.
(d) 16th. October 1683. John Earle. (Remainder torn away.)

(a) B. (Number torn off.) Walter Cobham. co. Berks. Husbandman. 29.
(b) Joseph Bull of Rodderith, co. Surrey. Marriner.
(c) Island of (? Barbadoes). (Remainder torn away.)

Nos. to 368 missing.

(a) B.369. Wm. Fisher. co. of Middx. 21. X.
(b) John Clarke of London. Merchant.
(c) Virginia. 4. Duke of Yorke. Capt. John Purvis.
(d) 17th. October 1683. John Butterwick. (Remainder torn away.)

(*a*) B.371. Wm. Howlett. co. Middx. 16.
(*b*) Christopher Deane of London. Merchant.
(*c*) Virginia. 7. Barnaby. Capt. Mathew Ryder.
(*d*) 17th. October 1683. John Butterick. (Abra. Bayly. Ro: Hastings.)

(*a*) B.372. James Jones. co. Middx. 21. Signs.
(*b*) Christopher Deane of London. Merchant.
(*c*) Virginia. 4. Barnaby. Capt. Mathew Ryder.
(*d*) 18th. October 1683. Daniell Briscoe. Richard Waring. (Abra. Bayly.)

(*a*) B. (Number torn off.) James Johnson. co. Middx. 22. X.
(*b*) Christopher Deane of London. Merchant.
(*c*) Virginia. . . . (blank) Barnaby. Capt. Mathew Ryder.
(*d*) 17th. October 1683. John Earle. (Abra. Bayly.)

(*a*) A. 374. Theophilus Wiloby (Willoby elsewhere). 19. X.
(*b*) John Clarke.
(*c*) Merryland. 6.
(*d*) 22nd. October 1683. Jon. Ingham. (Abra. Bayly. Ro: Hastings.)

(*a*) B.375. James Ellitt. co. Middx. 22. Signs James Elliott.
(*b*) Christopher Deane of London. Merchant.
(*c*) Virginia. 4. Barnaby. Capt. Mathew Ryder.
(*d*) 22nd. October 1683. Jon. Ingham. (Abra. Bayly.)

(*a*) A.376. Wm. Morres. 18. Signs William Moors.
(*b*) James Emmerson of parish of Stepney. Marriner.
(*c*) Virginia. 4.
(*d*) 22nd. October 1683. Jon. Ingham. (Abra. Bayly. Ro: Hastings.)

(*a*) B.377. Robt. Steele. co. Middx. Taylor. 21. X.
(*b*) Francis Lee of London. Merchant.
(*c*) Virginia. 4. Duke of Yorke. Capt. John Purvis.
(*d*) 23rd. October 1683. Jon. Ingham. (Abra. Bayly.)

(*a*) B.378. Joseph Peisley (?) co. Middx. Accomptant. 24. Signs Joseph Priestley.
(*b*) Wm. Howeland of London. Merchant.
(*c*) Virginia. 4. To serve as an Accomptant. Duke of Yorke. Capt. John Purvis.
(*d*) 25th. October 1683. Jon. Ingham. (Abra. Bayly.)

(*a*) B.379. John Bowles. co. Middx. 22. X.
(*b*) Christopher Deane of London. Merchant.
(*c*) Virginia. 4. Burnaby. Capt. Mathew Ryder.
(*d*) 25th. October 1683. Jon. Ingham. (Abra. Bayly.)

(a) B.380. Edmund Rice (?) co. Middx. 21. X.
(b) Christopher Deane of London. Merchant.
(c) Virginia. 4. Burnaby. Capt. Mathew Ryder.
(d) 25th. October 1683. Jon. Ingham. (Abra. Bayly.)

(a) B.381. Joseph Betts. co. Middx. 22. X.
(b) John Smith of London. Merchant.
(c) Virginia. 4. Virginia " furtop " (?) Capt. John Hill.
(d) 26th. October 1683. John Butterick. John Petman. (Abra. Bayly.)

(a) B. (Number torn off.) David Lewis. co. Middx. 18. X.
(b) John Clarke of London. Merchant.
(c) Virginia. 7. Unicorne. Capt. Norrington.
(d) 20th. October 1683. Jon. Ingham. (Abra. Bayly. Ro: Hastings.)

(a) B.383. Francis Farrow. co. Middx. 16. X.
(b) Edmund Putman of London. Merchant.
(c) Mariland. 8. Mary. Capt. Tippett.
(d) 31st. October 1683. Jon. Ingham. (Abra. Bayly. Cha. Osborne.)

(a) A.384. Eliz. Selnister. 16. X.
(b) John Purvis.
(c) Virginia. 6.
(d) 2nd. November 1683. Jon. Ingham. (Abra. Bayly.)
Ye sd. Eliz. Selnister made oath that her father & mother are ded & that she hath noe frind or Relations Liveinge.

(a) B.385. Mathew Greene. co. Middx. 16. X.
(b) Edmund Puttman of London. Merchant.
(c) Virginia. 8. Charles. Capt. Daniel Bird.
(d) 3rd. November 1683. Jon. Ingham. (Abra. Bayly. Cha. Osborne.)

(a) B.386. Nich. Easton. co. Middx. 21. X.
(b) Wm. Haveland of London. Merchant.
(c) Virginia. 4. Charles. Capt. Daniel Bird.
(d) 5th. Novr. 1683. Jon. Ingham. (Abra. Bayly.)

(a) B.387. John Stansell. co. Middx. 21. Signs.
(b) Wm. Haveland of London. Merchant.
(c) Virginia. 4. Mary. Capt. Tippitt.
(d) 6th. Novr. 1683. Henry Neale. X The mark of John Trickett. (Abra. Bayly.)

(a) A.388. William Foredom. 22. X.
(b) Wm. Haveland.
(c) Virginia. 4.
(d) 6th. Novr. 1683. Jon. Ingham. (Abra. Bayly.)

(a) B.389. Evan Evans. co. Middx. 30.
(b) John Bennett of London. Merchant.
(c) Jamaica. 4. William. Capt. John Bennett.
(d) 7th. Novr. 1683. Jon. Ingham. (Abra. Bayly.)
£5 with him.

(a) A.390. Katherine Thompson. 22. Signs Catarine Thompson.
(b) Mathew Prince.
(c) Virginia. 4.
(d) 7th. Novr. 1683. Jon. Ingham. (Abra. Bayly.)

(a) A.391. Isaack Steele. 23. Signs Isaac Steel.
(b) Mathew Rider of Ratcliff. Mariner.
(c) Virginia. 4.
(d) 9th. Novr. 1683. Jon. Ingham. (Abra. Bayly.)

(a) B.392. Wm. Key. co. Middx. 21. X.
(b) John Bennett of London. Marriner & Merchant.
(c) Jamaica. 6. William. Capt. John Bennett.
(d) 10th. Novr. 1683. Jon. Ingham. (Abra. Bayly.)

(a) B.393. Thomas Wootton. co. Middx. 21. X.
(b) Wm. Haveland of London. Merchant.
(c) Virginia. 6. Judith. Capt. Tryin.
(d) 10th. Novr. 1683. Jon. Ingham. (Abra. Bayly.)
£10 with him.

(a) A.394. Hannah Miles. 18. X.
(b) John Bennett.
(c) Jamaica. 4.
(d) 12th. Novr. 1683. Jon. Ingham. (Abra. Bayly. Cha. Osborne.)

(a) B.395. Wm. Meade. co. Middx. 27. Signs.
(b) John Smith of London. Merchant.
(c) Virginia. 4. Mary. Capt. Tippitt.
(d) 12th. Novr. 1683. Jon. Ingham. (Abra. Bayly.)
£10 with him.

(a) B.396. John East. co. Middx. 19. X.
(b) John Norington of London. Marriner & Merchant.
(c) Merriland. 4. Unicorne. Capt. John Norington.
(d) 27th. Octr. 1683. Jon. Ingham. (Cha. Osborne. H. Myddleton.)

(a) C.397. Thomas Stevenes. X.
(b) John Norinton.
(c) Virginia. 7.
(d) 30th. October 1683. Edward Browne. (Cha. Osborne. Abra. Bayly.)

(a) A. (torn ? 398) Hannah Atkins. 21. X.
(b) Phillipp Gower.

(c) Jamaica. 4.
(d) 27th. October 1683. Tho. Esme (?) Mark of John Bell. (Thomas Smith.)

Nos. 399 to 413 missing.

(a) A.414. William Davis. 22. X.
(b) Francis Pain of Limehous. Marriner.
(c) Virginia. 4.
(d) 1st. December 1683. William Edwards. (Abra. Bayly.)

(a) A.415. George Ivory. X.
(b) Robert Adams and Ann his wife.
(c) Jamaica. 6.
(d) 3rd. December 1683. Mark of Henry Ellis and William . . . (?) Geo. Lawson. (Tho. Hariot.)

(a) B.416. Robert Hill. Middx. 23. X.
(b) Anthony Wallinger of London. Merchant.
(c) Barbadoes. 4. Wm. & Robert. Capt. Giles Bond.
(d) 3rd. December 1683. Jon. Ingham. (Abra. Bayly.)

(a) B.417. Wm. Whaley. Middx. 24. X.
(b) Anthony Wallinger of London. Merchant.
(c) Barbadoes. 4. Wm. & Robert. Capt. Giles Bond.
(d) 3rd. December 1683. £10 with him. Jon. Ingham. (Abra. Bayly.)

(a) B.418. Joseph Wilson. Middx. 21. Signs.
(b) Tobias Frare of London. Merchant.
(c) Barbadoes. 4. Wm. & Robert. Capt. Giles Bond.
(d) 4th. December 1683. John Buttewick. (Abra. Bayly.)

(a) B.419. Kabell Dibdon. Middx. 16. X.
(b) John Williams of London. Merchant.
(c) Virginia. 9. Judith. Capt. Trym.
(d) 6th. December 1683. Jon. Ingham. (Abra. Bayly. Ro: Hastings.)

(a) Handwritten form. 420. Richard Betham. Signs.
(b) Robert Russell of Stepney, Middx. Mar.
(c) Barbadoes. 6.
(d) 7th. December 1683. Jacob Malden. ...eikle. Joph. Stockwell. (Abra. Bayly. Ro: Hastings.)

Nos. 421 to 430 missing.

(a) B.431. John Kinsbury. London. 30. X.
(b) William Haveland of London. Merchant.
(c) Jamaica. 4.

(*d*) 15th. September (torn)   And to have ten days after his arrival to seek his Redemption. (Torn.)

(*a*) B.432. James Edwards. London. 20. Signs.
(*b*) James Randall of London. Esq.
(*c*) Mariland. 4.
(*d*) 6th. October 1683. Samuell Jones. (Tho. Rowe.)

(*a*) B.433. Robert Cooper. London. 16. Signs.
(*b*) Thomas Carey of London. Marriner & Merchant.
(*c*) Mariland. 8. Adventure. Capt. Thomas Carey.
(*d*) 8th. October 1683. William Price. Isaac Steel. (Tho. Rowe. Abra. Bayly.)

(*a*) B.434. Rachell Ethewe. London. Spinster. 22. X.
(*b*) Thomas Carey of London. Marriner & Merchant.
(*c*) Mariland. 4. Adventure. Capt. Tho. Carey.
(*d*) 8th. October 1683. William Price. (Tho. Rowe.)

(*a*) B.435. John Rogers & wife from London. Him aged 31 & Wife Hester aged 20. Both sign. (? their names written for them.)
(*b*) Wm. Phillipps of London. Marriner.
(*c*) Mariland. 4. Love. Capt. Wm. Phillipps.
(*d*) 10th. October 1683. (Tho. Rowe.)

(*a*) B.436. John Henry. London. Groome. 23. X.
(*b*) Thomas Carey of London. Mar. & Mercht.
(*c*) Mariland. 4. Adventure. Capt. Thomas Carey.
(*d*) 10th. October 1683. (Tho. Rowe.)

(*a*) B.437. Richd. Jones. London. 21. X.
(*b*) Thomas Carey of London. Mar. & Mercht.
(*c*) Mariland. 4. Adventure. Capt. Thomas Carey.
(*d*) 11th. October 1683. The mark of Edmund Pattman. (Tho. Rowe.)

(*a*) B.438. Charles Guy. London. 23. X.
(*b*) Thomas Carey of London. Mar. & Mcht.
(*c*) Mariland. 4. Adventure. Capt. Thomas Carey.
(*d*) 12th. October 1683. (Tho. Rowe.)

(*a*) B.439. Michael Askin. Middx. 22. Michall Ask. Signs. Endorsed "Unicorne, Richard Askyson."
(*b*) William Haveland of London. Merchant.
(*c*) Mariland. 4. Unicorne. Capt. Norrington.
(*d*) 15th. October 1683. £5 with him. William Price. (Tho. Rowe.)

(*a*) B.440. Jone Churchill. Middx. Darymaid. 26. X.
(*b*) William Haveland of London. Merchant.
(*c*) Mariland. 4. Mary. To serve as Dairymaid.
(*d*) 15th. October 1683. William Price. (Tho. Rowe.)

(*a*) B.441. Lydea Coaks. Middx. Spinster. 18. X.
(*b*) William Haveland of London. Merchant.
(*c*) Mariland. 4. Mary.
(*d*) 16th. October 1683. (Tho. Rowe.)

(*a*) B.442. Thomas Cattbury. Middx. 20. X.
(*b*) William Haveland of London. Merchant.
(*c*) Virginia. 7. Duke of York. Capt. John Purvis.
(*d*) 20th. October 1683. William Goodbourne. Richard Waring. (Tho. Rowe.)

(*a*) B.443. Henry Harbridge. Middx. 22. X.
(*b*) Christopher Deane of London. Merchant.
(*c*) Virginia. 4. Barnaby. Capt. Mathew Ryder.
(*d*) 20th. October 1683. Samuell Jones. (Tho. Rowe.)

(*a*) B.444. Robert Morton. Middx. Shippwright. 30. Signs.
(*b*) John Norrington of London. Merchant.
(*c*) Virginia. 4. Barnaby. Capt. Mathew Ryder. To serve as Shipwright.
(*d*) 31st. October 1683. (Tho. Rowe.)

(*a*) B.445. John Horne. Middx. Tanner. 32. X.
(*b*) William Haveland of London. Merchant.
(*c*) Virginia. 4. Duke of Yorke. Capt. John Purvis. To serve as Tanner.
(*d*) 22nd. October 1683. £10: 10 with him. (Tho. Rowe.)

(*a*) B.446. Christopher Morton. Middx. 18. X.
(*b*) John Purvis of London. Marr. & Mercht.
(*c*) Virginia. 8. Duke of York. Capt. John Purvis.
(*d*) 24th. October 1683. (Tho. Rowe. Abra. Bayly.)

(*a*) B.447. John Evered (?). Middx. 16. X.
(*b*) Wm. Haveland of London. Merchant.
(*c*) Mariland. 6. Mary. Capt. Tippett.
(*d*) 27th. October 1683. John Stephenson the father-in-law. Elizabeth Stephenson the Own Mother. (Tho. Rowe.)

(*a*) B.448. John Smith. Middx. 30. X.
(*b*) Wm. Haveland of London. Merchant.
(*c*) Mariland. 4. Charles. Capt. Daniell Bird.
(*d*) 3rd. November 1683. The marks of Richard Peppes and Nicholas King. (Tho. Rowe.)

(a) B.449. Anne Shipperson. Middx. Spinster. 21. X.
(b) Wm. Haveland of London. Merchant.
(c) Mariland. 4. Mary. Capt. Typpott.
(d) 5th. November 1683. Thomas Juet. Mark of Francis Cole (?) Samuell Jones. (Tho. Rowe.)

(a) A.450. John Lomax. 15. X.
(b) Robert Adams of Jamaico, Planter, and Ann his wife.
(c) Jamaico. 7.
(d) 13th. December 1683. Robert Smith. Geo. Lawson. (Tho. Hariot.)

(a) A.451. William Thomas. 24. X.
(b) William Webb of Raphamack in Virginia. Shipwright.
(c) Virginia. 4.
(d) 13th. September 1683. William Hastings. (Ro: Hastings.)

(a) Hand-written form. 452. Benjamin Cooper the son of John Cooper of the parish of St. Mary Magdalen, Bermondsey, co. Surrey. Victualer. Signs.
(b) William Cooper of the parish of Stebunheath alias Stepney, co. Middx. Merchant.
(c) Virginia. 4.
(d) 17th. September 1683. John Cooper (the father). Thomas Elwood. (W. Smyth. Ro: Hastings.)

(a) Hand-written form. 453. John Truell. Aged about 30 years. St. Leonards, Shoreditch, Middx. Blacksmith.
(b) William Dockwra of London. Mercht.
(c) Province of New Jersey in America. 4.
(d) 18th. September 1683. ..elford (?) Leonard Burley. (Ro: Hastings.) Both Joseph Trowell and Will. Dockwra sign. The following clause occurs. " and after the end of the said terme to give pay and allow unto the said John Truell one breeding Sow & Corn sufficient to sow Two Acres of Land, and also doth further Covenant and promise to set out unto him five and twenty acres of land, granting him a deed for the same, to hold unto him & his heirs for ever, only at the quit rent of two pence per acre per annum."

(a) A.454. Jone Young. 21. X.
(b) Thomas Sloper of Petuxten in Merriland. gent.
(c) Merriland. 4.
(d) 19th. September 1683. James Bayly. Wm. Hastings. (Ro: Hastings.)

(a) A.455. Martha Barton. 22. X.
(b) Thomas Sloper of Petuxten in Merriland. gen.
(c) Merriland. 4.

(d) 19th. September 1683. James Bayly. Wm. Hastings. (Ro: Hastings.)

(a) A.456. Mary Glover. 21. X.
(b) Thomas Sloper of Petuxten in Merriland. gent.
(c) Merriland. 4.
(d) 19th. September 1683. James Bayly. Wm. Hastings. (Ro: Hastings.)

(a) A.457. Mary Jenkins. 23. X.
(b) Francis Parsons. Stepney. Marriner.
(c) Virginia. 4.
(d) 20th. September 1683. Willm. Hastings. (Ro: Hastings.)

(a) A.458. John Wilson. 21. Signs.
(b) William Yorke. Stepney. Marriner.
(c) Virginia. 4.
(d) 20th. September 1683. Willm. Hastings. (Ro: Hastings.)

(a) A.460. Nicholas Rowlson. X.
(b) Joseph Paine.
(c) Merryland. 4.
(d) 29th. September 1683. Edward Goldham. (Ro: Hastings.)

(a) B461. Willm. Withers. London. Husbandman. 22. X.
(b) Nicholas Prym. London. Marriner & Merchant.
(c) Virginia. 4. Richd. & Elizabeth. Capt. Nicho. Prym.
(d) 29th. September 1683. John Bromhead. (Ro: Hastings.)

(a) A.462. Barbary Feild. 11. X.
(b) Thomas Boile of Jamicah. Chirurgeon.
(c) Jamicah. 4.
(d) 10th. October 1683. Willm. Hastings. (Ro: Hastings. Abra. Bayly.)

(a) A.463. Peter Johnson. 25. Signs.
(b) Matthew Trynion. St. Pauls, Shadwell, Middx. Marriner.
(c) Virginia. 4.
(d) 7th. November 1683. Willm. Hastings. (Ro: Hastings.)

(a) A.464. Humphry Dixon. 26. Signs.
(b) John Rennett of Wapping, Stepney. Marriner.
(c) Jamicha. 4.
(d) 10th. November 1683.

(a) B.465. Wm. Giles. Middx. Curryer. 28. X.
(b) Wm. Haveland. London. Merchant.
(c) Barbadoes. 4. Wm. & Robert. Capt. Giles Bond. To be employed as a Curryer.
(d) 5th. December 1683. John Person. John Earle. (Ro: Hastings.)

(a) B.466. Henry Underwood. Middx. A Farrier Smith. 28. X.
(b) Wm. Haveland. London. Merchant.
(c) Barbadoes. 4. Wm. & Robert. Capt. Giles Bond. To be employed as a Farrier Smith.
(d) 5th. December 1683. Wm. Hastings. (Ro: Hastings.)

(a) B.467. Thomas Kelton. Middx. Cordwayner. 22. Signs "Thomas Kellson."
(b) Wm. Haveland. London. Merchant.
(c) Jamaica. 4. William. Capt. John Bennet. To be employed as a Cordwayner.
(d) 7th. November 1683. Rich. James. (Ro: Hastings.)

(a) A.468. Henry Boddard. 22. X.
(b) Robert Russell. Stepney co. Middx. Marriner.
(c) Barbadoes. 4.
(d) 8th. December 1683. James ..... (?) Wm. Hastings. (Ro: Hastings.)

(a) A special form. 469. John Hennagin. 22. X.
(b) John Bennett.
(c) Jamaica. 3.
(d) 11th. December 1683. Wm. Smyth. Wm. Hastings. (Ro: Hastings.)

(a) B.470. Francis Colman. Middx. Ploughman. 30. Signs (?).
(b) Wm. Haveland. London. Merchant.
(c) Barbadoes. 4. Wm. & Robert. Capt. Giles Bond. To be employed as a Ploughman.
(d) 21st. December 1683. £5 with him. John Richards. (Ro: Hastings.)

(a) B.471. John Krim (or Kym). Middx. Smith. 23. X.
(b) Wm. Haveland. London. Merchant.
(c) Barbadoes. 4. Wm. & Robert. Capt. Giles Bond. To be employed as a Smith.
(d) 18th. December 1683. £10 with him. James Williams. John Richards. (Abra. Bayly.) "A weeks Liberty allowed next after his arrival for to seek his Redemption."

(a) B.472. Daniel Arundall. Middx. 23. X.
(b) Wm. Wrayford. London. Merchant.
(c) Meavis. 4. St. George. Capt. Thomas Dann.
(d) 18th. December 1683. Jon. Ingham. (Abra. Bayly.)

(a) B.473. Samuel Johnson. Middx. House Carpenter. 24. X.
(b) Wm. Haveland. London. Merchant.
(c) Barbadoes. 4. Wm. & Robert. Capt. Giles Bond. To be employed as a House Carpenter.
(d) 20th December 1683. £10 with him. John Richards. (Abra. Bayly.)

(*a*) B.474. Thomas Smith. Middx. 23. Signs.
(*b*) Wm. Wrayford. London. Merchant.
(*c*) Meavis. 4. St. George. Capt. Thomas Dunn.
(*d*) 21st. December 1683. Jon. Ingham. (Abra. Bayly.)

(*a*) B.475. Tho. Swann Middx. 23. Signs "Thomas Swan."
(*b*) Wm. Wrayford of London. Merchant.
(*c*) Meavis. 4. St. George. Capt. Thomas Dunn.
(*d*) 21st December, 1683. John Person. (Abra. Bayly.)

(*a*) B.476. Joseph Midleton. Middx. BlackSmith. 24. X.
(*b*) Wm. Haveland. London. Merchant.
(*c*) Barbadoes. 4. To serve as a Blacksmith. Wm. and Robert. Capt. Giles Bond.
(*d*) 2nd. January 1683. Jon. Ingham. (Abra. Bayly.)

(*a*) B.477. John Brittland. Middx. a Taylor. 21. X.
(*b*) Wm. Haveland. London. Merchant.
(*c*) Barbadoes. 4. To serve as a Tailor. Wm. and Robert. Capt. Giles Bond.
(*d*) 2nd. January 1683. Jon. Ingham. (Abra. Bayly.)

(*a*) B.478. Samuel Norman. Middx. 21. Signs "Samuell Norman".
(*b*) Wm. Haveland. London. Merchant.
(*c*) Barbadoes. 4. Wm. and Robert. Capt. Giles Bond.
(*d*) 2nd. January, 1683. John Richards. (Ro: Hastings.)

(*a*) B.479. Thomas Honywell. Middx. 18. X.
(*b*) Tho. Dunn. London. Marriner.
(*c*) Meavis or Barbadoes. 5. St. George. Capt. Thomas Dunn.
(*d*) 3rd. Jany, 1683 Jon. Ingham. Mark of William Honywell, his father. (Abr. Bayly. Ro: Hastings.)

(*a*) B.480. Wm. Symmons (Simons elsewhere). Middx. 21. X.
(*b*) Thomas Dunn. London. Marriner.
(*c*) Meavis. 4. St. George. Capt. Thomas Dunn.
(*d*) 5th. January, 1683. Jon. Ingham. (Abra. Bayly.)

(*a*) B.481. John Seddich. Middx. Bricklayer. 22. X.
(*b*) Wm. Haveland. London. Merchant.
(*c*) Barbadoes. 4. To serve as a Bricklayer. Wm. and Robert. Capt. Giles Bond.
(*d*) 14th. January, 1683. £40 with him. Jon. Ingham. (Abra. Bayly.)

(*a*) B.482. Tho. Paine. Ploughman. co. Glost.(?) son of Tho. Paine deceased of Norledge. 21. X.
(*b*) Sr. Peter Collington Knt. of London. Merchant.
(*c*) Barbadoes. 4. To serve as a Ploughman. Wm. and Robert. Capt. Giles Bond.
(*d*) 16th. January, 1683. John Earle. (Abra. Bayly.)

(a) B.483. Abraham Ricky from Norwich and countie of ye same, son of Isack Ricky. 21. X.
(b) Christopher Prissitt. London. Marriner.
(c) Barbadoes. 4. " Barbadoes Merchant ", Capt. Christopher Prissitt.
(d) 28th. January, 1683. Jon Ingham. (Abra. Bayly.)

(a) B.484. James Gray. Haddon and countie of Sumersett, son of John Gray, decd. 21. X.
(b) William Precept. London. Marriner.
(c) Barbadoes. 4. To serve as a Groom. " Barbadoes Merchant ", Capt. Wm. Precept.
(d) 21st January, 1683. Jon. Ingham. (Abra. Bayly.)

(a) B.485. Andrew Ashley. Roso (?) and countie of Stafford. Son of John Ashby (sic), D.D., (dec. ?). 24. X.
(b) Wm. Haveland. London. Merchant.
(c) Barbadoes. 4. To serve as a Taylor. Wm. and Robert. Capt. Giles Bond.
(d) 21st. January, 1683. Jon. Ingham. (Abra. Bayly.)

(a) B.486. Richard Pettie. Canterbury, co. Kent, son of John Petty deceased. 21. X.
(b) Christopher Prissett. London. Marriner.
(c) Barbadoes. 5. " Barbadoes Merchant ". Capt. Christopher Pressett.
(d) 22nd. January, 1683. Jon. Ingham. (Abra. Bayly.)

(a) B.487. Hugh Parkington. Rinohenty (?) and co. of Chester, son of George Parkinson. 22. Signs.
(b) Christopher Prissitt. London. Marriner.
(c) Barbadoes. 4. To serve as a Ploughman. " Barbadoes Merchant ". Capt. Christopher Prissitt.
(d) 24th. January, 1683. Jon. Ingham. (Abra. Bayly.)

(a) B.488. Richard Spurling, co. of Kent, son of Allexander Spurling. 17. X.
(b) Christopher Prissick, London. Marriner.
(c) Barbadoes. 5. " Barbadoes Merchant ". Capt. Christopher Prissick.
(d) 11th. February, 1683. John Earle. (Abra. Bayly. Ro: Hastings.)

(a) B.489. John Clapp. Cherrick and co. of Dorsett. Son of William Clapp. 19. Signs.
(b) Christopher Prissick. London. Marriner.
(c) Barbadoes. 5. " Barbadoes Merchant ". Capt. Christopher Prissick.
(d) 16th. February, 1683. Tho. Pattman. (W. Smyth. Abra. Bayly.)

(*a*) A.490. Thomas Greenlees, husbandman. States on oath " 21 years and upwards ". Signs.
(*b*) Christopher Prissick of the parish of St. Paul, Shadwell, and co. Middx. Marriner.
(*c*) Island of Barbadoes. 4.
(*d*) 16th. February, 1683/4. John French. X. of Charles Weymouth. James Smith. (Abra. Bayly.)

(*a*) B.491. Abell Batrum. Middx. 24. Signs.
(*b*) Christopher Pressick. London. Marriner.
(*c*) Barbadoes. 4. " Barbadoes Merchant ". Capt. Christopher Pressick.
(*d*) 18th. February, 1683. Wm. Hastings. (Ro: Hastings.)

(*a*) 492. A special form (same as No. 469). George Raham (signs " George Wrangham "). 19. Signs.
(*b*) Richard Batts.
(*c*) Barbadoes. 5.
(*d*) 18th. February, 1683. J. Boughton. (W. Smyth. H. Myddleton.)

(*a*) B.493. Robert White. Middx. 28. Signs.
(*b*) Christopher Prissick, London. Marriner.
(*c*) Barbadoes. 4. " Barbadoes Merchant ". Capt. Christopher Prissick.
(*d*) 18th. February, 1683. Wm. Hastings. (Ro: Hastings.)

(*a*) B.494. Henry fflack, Colchester, co. Essex. 21. X.
(*b*) Christopher Prissick, London. Marriner.
(*c*) Barbadoes. 5. " Barbadoes Merchant ". Capt. Christopher Prissick.
(*d*) 18th. February, 1683. Wm. Hastings. (Abra. Bayly.) Armorial Seal.

(*a*) A.495. Elizabeth Taubutt. 16. X. Examined before us two of his Maies. Justices of the peace for the county of Middx. upon Oath and she saith her father and Mother are dcd. and that she is willing to serve four years in barbadoes.
(*b*) Christopher Prissick.
(*c*) Barbadoes. 4.
(*d*) 20th. February, 1683. Jon. Ingham. (Abra. Bayly. Ro: Hastings.)

(*a*) A.496. Mary Rissie (?). 19. Signs.
(*b*) Christopher Prissick. Marriner. Saith " father and mother both dead ".
(*c*) Barbadoes. 4.
(*d*) 20th. February, 1683/4. Jon. Ingham. (Abra. Bayly. Ro: Hastings.)

(*a*) B.497. Charles Towell. co. Devon (? son of) Thomas Towell. 20. X.

(b) Christopher Pressick. London. Marriner.
(c) Barbadoes. 6. " Barbadoes Merchant ". Capt. Christopher Pressick.
(d) 20th. February, 1683. X of John Dix. Richard Waring. (Abra. Bayly.)

(a) B.498. John Rice. (? co. Lancaster.) Son of David Rice. 21. X.
(b) Christopher Pressick. London. Marriner.
(c) Barbadoes. 4. To be employed as a Distiller. " Barbadoes Merchant ". Capt. Christopher Pressick.
(d) 20th. February, 1683. X. of John Dix. Richard Waring. (Abra. Bayly.)

(a) A.499. Mary Burnley. 19. Signs.
(b) Christopher Prissick.
(c) Barbadoes. 4.
(d) 20th. February, 1683. Jon. Ingham. (Abra. Bayly. Ro: Hastings.) says on oath " her mother and father are decd ".

(a) B.500. Wm. Street. co. Middx. Glazier. 24. Signs.
(b) Christopher Pressick. London. Merchant.
(c) Barbadoes. 4. " Barbadoes Merchant ". Capt. Christopher Pressick.
(d) 21st. February, 1683. Jon. Ingham. (Abra. Bayly.)

(a) B.501. Henry Agar. co. Middx. Accomptant. 21. Signs.
(b) Christopher Pressick. London. Marriner.
(c) Barbadoes. 4. To work as an accomptant. " Barbadoes Merchant ". Capt. Christopher Pressick.
(d) 22nd. February, 1683. Jon. Ingham. (Abra. Bayly.)

(a) B.502. John Copis. Middx. Ribbin Weaver. 22. Signs. " John Colpis ".
(b) Christopher Pressick. London. Merchant and Marrer.
(c) Barbadoes. 4. " Barbadoes Merchant ". Capt. Christopher Pressick.
(d) 25th. February, 1683. X of James Williams. (Abra. Bayly.)

(a) 503. A special form (as No. 469). John Beddoe. 21. X.
(b) Richard Coning of Wapping, Stepney. Marriner.
(c) Jamicah. 4.
(d) 27th. February, 1683. Henry Gideon. Wm. Hastings. (Ro: Hastings.)

(a) B.504. Edward Heather. Petersfield, Hampshire. Joyner and Cabbenetmaker. 25. Signs.
(b) John Dix. London. Merchant.
(c) Barbadoes. 4. To work as a Joyner and Cabbenetmaker. Crowne. Capt. Craft.
(d) 27th. February, 1683. Jon. Ingham. (Abra. Bayly.)

(a) B.505. John Williams, Chester, co. Chester. Son of Connerigg Williams. 24. Signs.
(b) Wm. Haveland. London. Merchant.
(c) Barbadoes. 4. To work as a farrier smith. Crowne. Capt. Crofts.
(d) 28th. February, 1683. Richard Waring. £5 with him. (Ro: Hastings.)

(a) B.506. Henry Wilson, co. Middx. Groom. 23. X.
(b) Wm. Goodburne. London. Merchant.
(c) Barbadoes. 4. To be employed as a Groom. Crowne. Capt. Tho. Croft.
(d) 29th. February, 1683. £5 with him. Jon. Ingham. (Abra. Bayly.)

(a) A.507. Jacob Paice. 22. Signs.
(b) William George.
(c) Barbadoes. 4.
(d) 29th. February, 1683. Jon. Ingham. (Abra. Bayly.)

(a) B.508. George Mason. co. Oxford, son of Tho. Mason. 21. Signs.
(b) John Sanders of London. Merchant.
(c) Barbadoes. 4. Crowne. Capt. Croft.
(d) 3rd. March, 1683. Jon. Ingham. (Abra. Bayly.)

(a) B.509. George Brace. co. Hereford, son of George Brace. 24. X.
(b) James Williams, of London. Merchant.
(c) Barbadoes. 4. To work as a Wheelright and Carpenter.
(d) 3rd. March, 1683. Richard Waring. (Abra. Bayly.)

(a) B.510. John King. Middx. Accomptant. 26. Signs.
(b) John Pearson. London. Merchant.
(c) Barbadoes. 4. To work as an Accomptant. Crowne. Capt. Crowne.
(d) 3rd. March, 1683. Jon. Ingham. (Abra. Bayly.)

(a) B.511. John Ast. Cawson, co. Wilts. Son of John Ast. 24. X.
(b) John Shawe. London. Merchant.
(c) Barbadoes. 4. To work as a Sawyer. Crowne. Capt. Croft.
(d) 3rd. March, 1683. Richard Waring. (Abra. Bayly.)

(a) B.512. Wm. Greene. Middx. Ploughman. 21. X.
(b) John Jones. London. Merchant.
(c) Barbadoes. 4. To work as a Ploughman. Crowne. Capt. Croft.
(d) 4th. March 1683. Jon. Ingham. (Abra. Bayly.)

(*a*) A.513. Edward Powell. Carpenter. 30 or thereabouts. Signs.
(*b*) Richard Batt of Tower Hill, Gentleman.
(*c*) Barbadoes. 4.
(*d*) 4th. March 1683/4. Adam Turnbull. Henry Wood. Geo. Lawson. (Thomas Smith.)

(*a*) B.514. Banjamin Levens. Essex. Colchester (?) Son of Wm. Leavens. 21. X.
(*b*) John Dix. London. Merchant.
(*c*) Meavis and Antega. 4. George. Capt. Bridgman.
(*d*) 6th. March, 1683. Richard Waring. (Abra. Bayly.)

(*a*) B.515. Giles Haddock. Middx. Ploughman. 21. X.
(*b*) John Neale. London. Merchant.
(*c*) Jamaica. 4. To work as a Ploughman. Providence. Capt. Bartholomew.
(*d*) 6th. March 1683. Jon. Ingham. (Abra. Bayly.)

(*a*) B.516. John Rawlings. Middx. Sawyer. 27. X.
(*b*) John Norris. London. Merchant.
(*c*) Jamaica. 4. To work as a Sawyer. Providence. Capt. Bartholomew.
(*d*) 7th. March 1683. John Richards. (Ro: Hastings.)

(*a*) B.517. James Kimpson. Middx. Glaizer. 21. Signs " James Kimson."
(*b*) John Rowe. London. Merchant.
(*c*) Jamaica. 4. To work as a Glaizer. Providence. Capt. Bartholomew.
(*d*) 12th. March 1683. James Williams. (Abra. Bayly.)

(*a*) B.518. Humphry Martin. Devon. 27. X.
(*b*) John Rose. London. Merchant.
(*c*) Jamaica. 4. Providence. Capt. Bartholomew.
(*d*) 17th. March 1683. John Richards. (Ro: Hastings.)

(*a*) B.519. Robert Weston. Rye. Sussex. 22. X.
(*b*) Thomas Wise. London. Merchant.
(*c*) Antega. 4. Francis & Dorothy. Capt. Richard Bridgman.
(*d*) 17th. March 1683. Thomas Pattmain. John Shaw. (Abra. Bayly.)

(*a*) A.520. Wm. Phillips. 27. Signs " William Phillippes."
(*b*) Edmund Paine of Stepney. Marriner.
(*c*) Pencillvainia. 4.
(*d*) 19th. March 1683. Jon. Ingham. (Abra. Bayly.)

(*a*) B.521. Zachariah Gray. Middx. Ploughman. 22. (Does not sign. No mark.)
(*b*) Richard Waterhowse. London. Merchant.

(c) Jamaica. 4. To serve as a Ploughman. Providence. Capt. Bartholomew.
(d) 24th. March 1683. (No witness) (Abra. Bayly.)

(a) A.522. Dorothy Hutchinson. 21. Spinster. X.
(b) John Humphryes. East Smithfield. Marriner.
(c) Jamaicha. 4.
(d) 29th. March 1684. Wm. Hastings. (Ro: Hastings.)

(a) A.523. Elizabeth Wilkinson. Spinster. 21. X.
(b) John Humphreys. East Smithfield. Marriner.
(c) Jamicha. 4.
(d) 29th. March 1684. Wm. Hastings. (Ro: Hastings.)

(a) B.524. Joseph Sparkes. Willner co. Stafford. Smith. 23. X.
(b) John Stone. London. Merchant.
(c) Jamaica. 4. To serve as a Smith. Providence. Capt. Bartholomew.
(d) 29th. March 1684. £2:6 with him. Richard Waring. William Goodburn. (Abra. Bayly.)

(a) B.525. Wm. Whiting. Hurkett co. Northampton. Son of Wm. Whiting. 21. X.
(b) John Wiseman. London. Merchant.
(c) Jamaica. 4. To serve as Husbandman. George. Capt. Jones.
(d) 29th. March 1684. Richard Waring. (Abra. Bayly.)

(a) B.526. Richard Holt. Burnidge co. Lancaster. Groom. 23. Signs.
(b) John Wiseman. London. Merchant.
(c) Jamaica. 4. To serve as a Groom. George. Capt. Jones.
(d) 1st. April 1684. John Person. (Abra. Bayly.)

(a) B.527. Tho: Burton. Bixtons (?) co. Lincolne. 24. Signs.
(b) John Hall. London. Merchant.
(c) Antega. 4. To serve as an Accomptant. Anne & Mary. Capt. Harvey.
(d) 3rd. April 1684. John Newson. (Abra. Bayly.)

(a) B.528. Tho. Dyer. Pangburne co. Berks. 20. X.
(b) John Hall. London. Merchant.
(c) Antega. 4. Anne & Mary. Capt. Isaack Harvey.
(d) 4th. April 1684. Samuell Barker. (Abra. Bayly. Ro: Hastings.)

(a) B.529. John Owene. Middx. 22. X.
(b) John Williams. London. Merchant.
(c) Barbadoes. 4. Wm. & Robert. Capt. Giles Bond.
(d) 28th. December 1683. Ob. Reynolds. (Tho: Cheek.)

(a) B.530. Wm. Haye (?Hope). Cranbrooke, Kent. Son of Andro (?Antho.) ?Hope. 21. X.

(*b*) Harke Garbrane. London. Merchant.
(*c*) Jamaica. 4. George. Capt. Jones.
(*d*) 23rd. March 1683. Juthe (?) Preseme. (Tho: Cheek.)

(*a*) B.531. John Solley. Ash. Kent. Son of Tho: Solly. 21. X.
(*b*) Harke Garbrane. London. Merchant.
(*c*) Jamaica. 4. George. Capt. Jones.
(*d*) 23rd. March 1684. (No witness) (Tho: Cheek.)

(*a*) C.532. John Smith. London. Shoemaker. 28. Signs.
(*b*) Thomas Richardson. Chururgeon. London.
(*c*) Island of Jamaica. 4.
(*d*) 26th. March 1684. Ob. Reynolds. (Tho: Cheek.)

(*a*) C.533. Jane Whitfield. Alston More. Cumberland. Spinster. 21. X.
(*b*) Thomas Richardson. Citizen & Chururgeon of London.
(*c*) Island of Jamaica. 4.
(*d*) 28th. March 1684. Thomas Ellis. George Lehunt. (Tho: Cheek.)

(*a*) C.534. Margarett Jones of Waterford in the Kingdom of Ireland. 22. Signs " Margret Jones ".
(*b*) Thomas Richardson. Citizen & Chururgeon of London.
(*c*) Island of Jamaica. 4.
(*d*) 28th. March 1684. Ob. Reynolds. (Tho: Cheek.)

(*a*) C.535. Alice Duckett. Pembridge. co. Hereford. Widow. 24. X.
(*b*) George Lehunt. Citizen & Merchant of London.
(*c*) Island of Jamaica. 4.
(*d*) 28th. March 1684. Thomas Richardson. Thomas Ellis. (Tho: Cheek.)

(*a*) C.536. Mary fflack. Portsmouth. co. Southton. Widow. 22. X.
(*b*) George Lehunt. Citizen & Merchant of London.
(*c*) Island of Jamaica. 4.
(*d*) 28th. March 1684. Tho: Richardson. Thomas Ellis. (Tho: Cheek.)

(*a*) B.537. Patrick Sasfield. Gyles in the Fields. Middx. Barber. 21. Signs " Patrick Sarsfield ".
(*b*) John Hill. London. Merchant.
(*c*) Antega. 4. To serve as a Barber. Anne & Mary. Capt. Isaack Harvey.
(*d*) 8th. April 1684. Randte (?) Murton (?). (Abra. Bayly.)

(*a*) B. 538. George Preston. Tositer (Towcester) Northampton. 21. Signs.

- (*b*) John Jones. London. Marriner.
- (*c*) Carolenia. 4. Joseph & Ashton. Capt. John Jones.
- (*d*) 14th. April 1684. Geo. Hill. (Abra. Bayly.)

- (*a*) B.539. John fford. Wootton under Edge. co. Glos. Weaver. 21. X.
- (*b*) John Hall. London. Merchant.
- (*c*) Barbadoes. 4. To be employed as a Weaver if there used. John & Elizabeth. Capt. Jonas Leech.
- (*d*) 19th. April 1684. John Farr (?). Samuell Barker. (Abra. Bayly.)

- (*a*) B.540. Tho: Heyward. Oare. co. Sussex. Ploughman. 22. X.
- (*b*) John Hall. London. Merchant.
- (*c*) Barbadoes. 4. To serve as a Ploughman. John & Elizabeth. Capt. Jonas Leech.
- (*d*) 21st. April 1684. Tho: Pattman. Richard Waring. (Abra. Bayly.)

- (*a*) B.541. Henry Wilson. Aderston. co. Warwick. Groom. 21. Signs.
- (*b*) John Hall. London. Merchant.
- (*c*) Barbadoes. 4. To serve as a Groom. John & Elizabeth. Capt. Jonas Leech.
- (*d*) 22nd. April 1684. John Williams. (Abra. Bayly.)

- (*a*) B.542. Tho: Rowland. co. Mountgomery. 21. X.
- (*b*) George Smith. London. Merchant.
- (*c*) Jamaica. 4. To serve as a Husbandman. Richard & Sarah. Capt. Thomas Stubbs.
- (*d*) 25th. April 1684. James Williams. (Abra. Bayly.)

- (*a*) B.543. James Swain. Coggs. co. Oxon. 21. Signs.
- (*b*) Thomas Stubbs. London. Merchant.
- (*c*) Jamaica. 4. Richard & Sarah. Capt. Thomas Stubbs.
- (*d*) 28th. April 1684. John Dix. Robert Preston. (Abra. Bayly.)

- (*a*) B.544. James Thorp. Uppingham. co. Rutland. Miller. 21. X.
- (*b*) John Smith. London. Merchant.
- (*c*) Jamaica. 4. To serve as a Miller. Richard & Sarah. Capt. Thomas Stubbs.
- (*d*) 1st. May 1684. £5 with him. John Richards. (Abra. Bayly.)

- (*a*) B.545. Hugh Sneath. St. Martins in the co. of Middx. Vintner. 28. Signs.
- (*b*) John Smith. London. Merchant.
- (*c*) Barbadoes. 4. To serve as a Vintner. Friendshipp. Capt. Wm. Bedding.
- (*d*) 1st. May 1684. Robert ffudge. (Abra. Bayly.)

(a) A.546. Elizabeth Ivory. 23. X.
(b) William Orton of Ratclif. Marriner.
(c) Carolina. 4.
(d) 1st. May 1684. John Cooke. (Abra. Bayly.)

(a) B.547. Joseph Pagrame (?) Bloyfield. co. Norfolk. Gardener. 21. X.
(b) John Smith. London. Merchant.
(c) Jamaica. 4. To serve as a Gardener. Richard & Sarah. Capt. Thomas Stubbs.
(d) 1st. May 1684. £5 with him. John Richards. (Abra. Bayly.)

(a) A.548. Benjamin Porter. 21. Signs "Benj. Porter".
(b) Edmond Pain. London. Merchant.
(c) Pensilvaina. 4.
(d) 2nd. May 1684. Mark of Lewis Kvia. (Abra. Bayly.)

(a) B.549. Francis Pearse. Bridg Norton. co. Glos. Husbandman. 21. Signs.
(b) William Haveland. London. Merchant.
(c) Barbadoes. 4. To serve as a Husbandman. Friendshipp. Capt. Wm. Bedding.
(d) 7th. May 1684. William goodbourne. (Abra. Bayly.)

(a) B.550. Benjamin Maple. Ipswich. co. Suffolk. 21. X.
(b) John Smith. London. Merchant.
(c) Barbadoes. 4. To serve as a Husbandman. Friendshipp. Capt. Wm. Bedding.
(d) 8th. May 1684. William goodbourne. (Abra. Bayly.)

(a) B.551. George Parsons. From the county of Salop. Ploughman. 21. X.
(b) William Haveland. London. Merchant.
(c) Barbadoes. 4. To serve as a Ploughman. Friendshipp. Capt. Wm. Bedding.
(d) 12th. May 1684. (No witness) (Abra. Bayly.)

(a) A.552. Richard Nibbs. 32. X.
(b) William Orton. Radclif. Marriner.
(c) Virginia or Carolinia. 4.
(d) 17th. May 1684. Mark of John Shaw. (Abra. Bayly.)

A new form of printed Indenture now appears. It is only slightly different in wording from form "B" so we do not propose to print it in full. It will be marked "D".

(a) D.553. William Printice son of Wm. Printice from Lotten (Latton) co. Essex. 25. X.
(b) William Haveland. London. Merchant.
(c) Barbadoes. 4. Friendshipp. Capt. William Bedding.
(d) 20th. May 1684. George Hill. (Abra. Bayly.)

(*a*) A.554. Robert Tasker. 21. X.
(*b*) William Smyth. Wappen. co. Middx. Marriner.
(*c*) Pensilvania. 4.
(*d*) 23rd. May 1684. Tho. Butler. (Abra. Bayly.)

(*a*) D.555. John Passmore son of John Passmore from Exon. co. Devon. About 22. Chirurgion. Signs with a bold signature.
(*b*) John Jones. London. Merchant.
(*c*) Barbadoes. 4. To serve as a Chirurgion. Friendshipp. Capt. William Bedding.
(*d*) 27th. May 1684. James Williams. (Abra. Bayly.)

(*a*) D.556. Francis Poole son of Mathew Poole deceased from Northampton in the county of the same. About 29. A Husbandman. Signs.
(*b*) William Haveland. London. Merchant.
(*c*) Barbadoes. 4. To serve as a Husbandman. Friendshipp. Capt. William Bedding.
(*d*) 28th. May 1684. Richard Hunt. Richard Hicks. (Abra. Bayly.)

(*a*) D.557. Thomas Herick son of Wm. Herick from Woodhouse. co. Leicester. 21. Gent. Signs " Thomas Herricke."
(*b*) William Haveland. London. Merchant.
(*c*) Barbadoes. 4. Friendshipp. Capt. William Bedding.
(*d*) 28th. May 1684. Richard Hunt. Richard Hicks. (Abra. Bayly.)

(*a*) D.558. Obediah Buck son of James Buck from the city of Wells. co. Summersett. About 27. A Girdler. By consent of Heneretta his wife. Signs " Obadiah Buck."
(*b*) William Haveland. London. Merchant.
(*c*) Barbadoes. 4. To serve as a Girdler if there used. Friendshipp. Capt. William Bedding.
(*d*) 30th. May 1684. Henerita Buck. John Richards. (Abra. Bayly.)

(*a*) D.559. Daniel Church son of James Church from Hempstead. co. Hertford. About 23. A Turner. X.
(*b*) William Haveland. London. Merchant.
(*c*) Barbadoes. 4. To serve as a Turner. Friendshipp. Capt. Wm. Bedding.
(*d*) 30th. May 1684. John Richards. (Abra. Bayly.)

(*a*) D.560. George Price (called Gregory twice in the Indenture) son of John Price, deceased, from Bonthored (?) co. Hereford. 24. Labourer. X.
(*b*) Richard Batts. London. Merchant.
(*c*) Jamaica. 4. To serve as a Labourer. William & Mary. Capt. Mingiam.
(*d*) –May 1684. Joseph Foy. (Abra. Bayly.)

(a) D.561. Thomas Lodge. A Ploughman. About 21. From Cletheroe, co. Lancs. Son of John Lodge, deceased. X.
(b) John Browne. London. Merchant.
(c) Jamaica. 4. To serve as a Ploughman. William & Mary. Capt. Mingiam.
(d) 4th. June 1684. Richard Waring. (Abra. Bayly.)

(a) A.562. Thomas Foller. 21. X.
(b) David Carr. London. Marriner.
(c) Virginia or Carolina. 4.
(d) 6th. June 1684. Christopher Osburne. (Abra. Bayly.)

(a) D.563. William Hippy. A Labourer. About 21. Derrington. co. Northampton. X.
(b) John Browne. London. Merchant.
(c) Jamaica. 4. William & Mary. Capt. Mingiam.
(d) 9th. June 1684. James Williams. (Abra. Bayly.)

(a) A.564. William Thomson. 21. X.
(b) David Carr. London. Marriner.
(c) Virginia or Carolinia. 4.
(d) 12th. June 1684. Christopher Baylif. (Abra. Bayly.)

(a) D.565. Thomas Crampton son of John Crampton from Manchester, co. Lancs. About 22. A Husbandman. Signs.
(b) Henry Tragany. London. Merchant.
(c) Mariland. 4. Brothers Adventure. Capt. Henry Tragany.
(d) 12th. June 1684. John Cooke. (Abra. Bayly.)

(a) D.566. John Bird son of Edward Bird from Shafston. co. Dorset. About 21. A Cordwayner. Signs " John Burd ".
(b) John Bright. London. Merchant.
(c) Virginia. 4. To serve as a Cordwayner. Booth. Capt. Peter Pagan.
(d) 19th. June 1684. £5 with him. Edward Pattman. (Abra. Bayly.)

(a) D.567. Elizabeth Skipp. About 21. Eastsmithfield. co. Middx. Daughter of Francis Skipp deceased. Spinster. Now apprenticed. X.
(b) John Bright. London. Merchant.
(c) Virginia. 4. Booth. Capt. Peter Pagan.
(d) 12th. June 1684. Samuell Barker. (Abra. Bayly.)

(a) D.568. Thomas Howorth son of James Howorth. Haslrigden. co. Lancs. About 21. A Weaver. Signs.
(b) John Bright. London. Merchant.
(c) Virginia. 4. Booth. Capt. Peter Pagan.
(d) 24th. June 1684. John Bellme. (Abra. Bayly.)

(a) D.569. Wm. Scarr son of Arther Scarr, from Algate High. co. Middx. About 26. A Labourer. Originally from Ireland. X.
(b) John Bright. London. Merchant.
(c) Virginia. 4. To serve as a Labourer. Booth. Capt. Peter Pagan.
(d) 20th. June 1648. John Person. (Abra. Bayly.)

(a) D.570. John Hannam son of John Hannam from Dorchester in the county of the same. About 21. X.
(b) John Bright. London. Merchant.
(c) Virginia. 4. To serve as a Labourer. Booth. Capt. Peter Pagan.
(d) 21st. June 1684. John Person. (Abra. Bayly.)

(a) B.571. Robert Abell. co. Middx. A Sawyer. 28. Signs.
(b) John Pearson. London. Merchant.
(c) Antego. 4. To serve as a Sawyer. Francis & Dorathy. Capt. Bridgman.
(d) 11th. March 1683. (No witness) (Cha. Osborne. Ro: Hastings.)

(a) B.572. John Rachell. co. Middx. 21. X.
(b) James Moore. London. Merchant.
(c) Jamaica. 4. George. Capt. Jones.
(d) 25th. March 1683. (No witness) (Cha. Osborne.)

(a) B.573. Tho. Dymond. Leeds. co. York. 21. Signs.
(b) Wm. Jones. London. Merchant.
(c) Barbadoes. 4. Katherine. Capt. Emberly.
(d) 24th. March 1683. William Baily. (Cha. Osborne.)

(a) B.574. Francis Wardle. co. Chester. Husbandman. 22. X.
(b) William Somes. London. Merchant.
(c) Jamaica. 4. To serve as a Husbandman. George. Capt. Jones.
(d) 25th. March 1683. Tho: Pattinson. (Cha. Osborne.)

(a) B.575. John Seethings. Banham. co. Norfolk. 21. Signs.
(b) Wm. Jones. London. Merchant.
(c) Barbadoes. 4. Katherine. Capt. Emberly.
(d) 24th. March 1683. Thomas Dymond. (Cha. Osborne.)

(a) B.576. Richard Reynelds, from Bristol. Son of Richard Reynolds. 21. Signs "Richard Raynalls".
(b) John Hill. London. Merchant.
(c) Antego. 4. Anne & Mary. Capt. Isaack Harvey.
(d) –April 1684. John Huxford. (Cha. Osborne.)

(a) B.577. George Bryant. Lester. co. Leicester. Weaver. 25. Signs.
(b) John Hall. London. Merchant.

(c) Barbadoes. 4. To serve as a Weaver if there used. John & Elizabeth. Capt. Jonas Leech.
(d) 19th. April 1684. George Hill. (Cha. Osborne.)

(a) B.578. Richd. Kilner (called Killmor elsewhere). co. Westmerland. A Labourer. 25. X.
(b) William Haveland. London. Merchant.
(c) Barbadoes. 4. To serve as a Labourer. Friendshipp. Capt. Wm. Bedding.
(d) 26th. April 1684. Richard Tarling. (Cha. Osborne.)

(a) B.579. Joshua Browne. Hallifax. co. York. Clothier. 26. X.
(b) William Haveland. London. Merchant.
(c) Barbadoes. 4. To serve as " what he is fit for ". Friendshipp. Capt. Wm. Bedding.
(d) 28th. April 1684. Charles Hartley. Ely Bentley. (Cha. Osborne.)

(a) C.580. John White. Parish of Allgate. 15. X.
(b) John Turpin. Waping, White Chappell. Mariner.
(c) Barbadoes. 6.
(d) 12th. May 1684. Edward Browne. Mark of Thomas Wellford Cha. Osborne. (Abra. Bayly.)

(a) D.581. Walter Hooper son of Walter Hooper. Atherley. Gloucestershire. 23. A Glayzer. Signs.
(b) William Haveland. London. Merchant.
(c) Barbadoes. 4. To serve as a Glazyer. Friendshipp. Capt. William Bedding.
(d) 16th. May 1684. Mark of Edmund Patman. (Cha. Osborne.)

(a) C.582. William Pearson. Cittyson. 22. Signs.
(b) William Beeding. Wapping. Marriner. co. Middx.
(c) Barbadoes. 4.
(d) 4th. June 1684. Edw. Browne. John Seele. (Cha. Osborne.)

(a) D.583. Thomas Sclater son of Henry Sclater. London. 18. Signs.
(b) Sr. Peter Collington Knt. London. Merchant.
(c) Barbadoes. 4. Friendshipp. Capt. William Bedding.
(d) 7th. June 1684. Nathanell Collings. John Berry. (Abra. Bayly.)

(a) D.584. Thomas Lestrange son of Thomas Lestrange. Woodbridge. co. Suffolk. About 29. Accomptant. Signs.
(b) Henry Tragany. London. Merchant.
(c) Mariland. 4. Brothers Adventure. Capt. Henry Tragany.
(d) 14th. June 1684. Edw. Browne. (Cha. Osborne.)

(a) D.585. Cornelius Campion son of Michael Campion. Thackford. co. Essex. About 27. A Barber. Signs.

(b) John Jones. London. Merchant.
(c) Jamaica. 4. To serve as a Barber. Wm. & Mary. Capt. Mingnon.
(d) 17th. June 1684. Tho. Pattman. John Richards. (Cha. Osborne.)

(a) D.586. John Whithead son of Thomas Whiting (sic.). Ubley. co. Somerset. About 21. A Barber. Signs "John Whiteside".
(b) John Bright. London. Merchant.
(c) Virginia. 4. To serve as a Barber. Booth. Capt. Peter Pagan.
(d) 23rd. June 1684. Richard Merren. (Abra. Bayly.)

(a) D.587. William Tompson son of William Tompson. Huttingham (?) Cambridgeshire. About 21. A Husbandman. Signs.
(b) John Bright. London. Merchant.
(c) Virginia. 4. To serve as a Husbandman. Booth. Capt. Peter Pagan.
(d) 23rd. June 1684. James Williams. William goodbourne. (Abra. Bayly.)

(a) D.588. William Holmes son of Wm. Holmes. St. Eedes. co. Huntingdon. About 21. A Labourer. X.
(b) John Bright. London. Merchant.
(c) Virginia. 4. To serve as a Labourer. Booth. Capt. Peter Pagan.
(d) 23rd. June 1684. John Dix. John Cock. (Abra. Bayly.)

(a) D.589. William Whiting son of Thomas Whiting. St. Clements Danes, co. Middx. About 20. Accomptant. Signs.
(b) Wm. Haveland. London. Merchant.
(c) Barbadoes. 4. To serve as an Accomptant. Prince. Capt. Jonathan Wilson.
(d) 23rd. June 1684. Tho. Ashton. John Richards. (Abra. Bayly.)

(a) D.590. Symon Leeson son of Benjamin Leeson. Hartpool. co. Hertford. About 21. A Taylor. X.
(b) James Williams. London. Merchant.
(c) Virginia. 4. To serve as a Taylor. Prince. Capt. Jonathan Wilson.
(d) 23rd. June 1684. (No witness) (Abra. Bayly.)

(a) D.591. John Elderkin son of John Elderkin. St. Peters Allwinckle. co. Northampton. About 25. A Groom. X.
(b) John Bright. London. Merchant.
(c) Virginia. 4. To serve as a Groom. Booth. Capt. Peter Pagan.
(d) 23rd. June 1684. Edmund Pattinan. (Abra. Bayly.)

(a) D.592. John Porter son of George Porter. Isle of Ely. co. Cambridge. About 22. Signs.

(*b*) John Bright. London. Merchant.
(*c*) Virginia. 4. Booth. Capt. Peter Pagan.
(*d*) 24th. June 1684. John Person. (Abra. Bayly.)

(*a*) A.593. Thomas York. 21. X.
(*b*) Peter Peake. London. Mariner.
(*c*) Maryland. 4.
(*d*) 24th. June 1684. John Williams. (Abra. Bayly.)

(*a*) D. 594. Mary Saly. Kirton. co. Devon. Daughter of George Saly. Spinster. 26. X.
(*b*) John Bright. London. Merchant.
(*c*) Virginia. 4. Booth. Capt. Peter Pagan.
(*d*) 24th. June 1684. John Richards. 51s. (?£) with her. (Abra. Bayly.)

(*a*) D. 595. Richard Peatey, son of John Peatey. Canterbury. co. Kent. Labourer. 22. Signs " Richard Peaty."
(*b*) John Bright. London. Merchant.
(*c*) Virginia. To serve as a Labourer. (period not stated) Booth. Capt. Peter Pagan.
(*d*) 25th. June 1684. Edmund Patterson. (Abra. Bayly.)

(*a*) D.596. Sammell Ratcliff, son of Wm. Ratclife. Miller. co. Derby. Husbandman. 24. X.
(*b*) John Bright. London. Merchant.
(*c*) Virginia. 4. To serve as a Husbandman. Booth. Capt. Peter Pagan.
(*d*) 26th. June 1684. Wm. Dix. William goodbourne. (Abra. Bayly.)

(*a*) A.597. Sarah Phillips. 21.
(*b*) Thomas Sweet. London. Mariner.
(*c*) Maryland. 4.
(*d*) 27th. June 1684. (Unsigned. No Witness or Magistrate.)

(*a*) D.598. Thomas Smeethes son of John Smeethes. Bowdley. co. Worster. Accomptant. 22. Signs.
(*b*) John Bright. London. Merchant.
(*c*) Virginia. 4. To serve as an Accomptant. Booth. Capt. Peter Pagan.
(*d*) 27th. June 1684. James Williams. (Abra. Bayly.)

(*a*) D.599. John Towne son of John Towne. Worminghall (?). Bucks. 18. X.
(*b*) John Bright. London. Merchant.
(*c*) Virginia. 7. Booth. Capt. Peter Pagan.
(*d*) 27th. June 1684. John Williams. (John Berry. Abra. Bayly.)

(*a*) A.600. Mary Spenser. 21.
(*b*) James Brayner. London. Merchant.

(c) Virginia. 4.
(d) 27th. June 1684. Mark of William Jennings. (Abra. Bayly.)

(a) D.601. Nathaniell Mayne. Coachman. Son of Nathaniell Mayne. Newton Bushell. co. Devon. Coachman. 21. Signs.
(b) Wm. Haveland. London. Merchant.
(c) Barbadoes. 4. To serve as a Coachman. Prince. Capt. Jonathan Wilson.
(d) 28th. June 1684. Tho. Pattinson. (Abra. Bayly.)

(a) B.602. John Thompson. co. Middx. Ploughman. 22. X.
(b) John Shawe. London. Merchant.
(c) Barbadoes. 4. To serve as a Ploughman. Katherine. Capt. Emberly.
(d) 4th. April 1684. Richard Waring. (Ro: Hastings.)

(a) B.603. Addam Gregory. co. Lancaster. 21. X.
(b) Sir Henry Johnson Knt. London. Merchant.
(c) Carolina. 4. Joseph & Ashton. Capt. John Jones.
(d) 4th. April 1684. Richard Waring. (Ro: Hastings.)

(a) B.604. John Law from the Kingdom of Scotland. 32. X.
(b) John Smith. London. Merchant.
(c) Carolina. 4. Joseph & Ashton. Capt. John Jones.
(d) 11th. April 1684. Richard Waring. (Ro: Hastings.)

(a) A.605. William Ford. 27. Signs "Will. fforde."
(b) Ransford Waterhouse. Wapping. Merchant.
(c) Jamaica. 4.
(d) 11th. April 1684. Wm. Hastings. (Ro: Hastings.)

(a) B.606. Richard Hicks. co. Montgomory. Accomptant. 26. Signs.
(b) John Smith. London. Merchant.
(c) Carolina. 4. To serve as an Accomptant. Joseph & Ashton. Capt. John Jones.
(d) 27th. April 1684. Richard Waring. (Ro: Hastings.)

(a) B.607. Elizabeth Merring. Town and co. of Notts. Spinster. 23. X.
(b) Daniell Heyward. London. Marriner.
(c) Antego. 4. Anne & Mary. Capt. Isaack Harvey.
(d) 18th. April 1684. Daniell Bristoe. (Ro: Hastings.)

(a) B.608. Thomas Savage. St. Clement's. co. Middx. Taylor. 24. Signs.
(b) John May. London. Merchant.
(c) Barbadoes. 4. To serve as a taylor. John & Elizabeth. Capt. Jonas Leech.
(d) 18th. April 1684. William goodbourne. (Ro: Hastings.)

(*a*) B.609. Richard Trelford. Kirkcome (?). co. Lancash. Smith. 26. X.
(*b*) Richard Batts. London. Merchant.
(*c*) Barbadoes. 4. To serve as a Blacksmith. Friendship. Capt. Wm. Bedding.
(*d*) 28th. April 1684. Tho: Hutchens. (Cha. Osborne.)

(*a*) A.610. Savile Jackson. 21. Signs.
(*b*) Nathaniell Taylor. Stepney. Marriner.
(*c*) Barbadoes. 4.
(*d*) 29th. April 1684. Wm. Hastings. (Ro: Hastings.)

(*a*) D.611. John Getchell son of John Getchell. Uphatch. co. Summersett. 19. Signs "John Gatchell."
(*b*) John Bright. London. Merchant.
(*c*) Virginia. 6. Booth. Capt. Peter Pagan.
(*d*) 3rd. June 1684. John Booth. (Abra. Bayly. Ro: Hastings.)

(*a*) D.612. Nicholas Barnes son of Henry Barnes. Norwich. co. same. 23. Labourer. X.
(*b*) John Bright. London. Merchant.
(*c*) Virginia. 4. To serve as a Labourer. Booth. Capt. Peter Pagan.
(*d*) 3rd. June 1684. Abraham Harrison. (Abra. Bayly.)

(*a*) D.613. John Lowdon (Lowdom?) Exon. co. Devon. 19. Shoemaker. Signs "John Lowdom."
(*b*) William Hutchens. London. Merchant.
(*c*) Maryland. 5. Brothers Adventure. Capt. Henry Tragany.
(*d*) 10th. June 1684. Tho. Wi . . . (?). (John Borry. Abra. Bayly.)

(*a*) D.614. Francis Haires son of Edward Haires. St. Pankridge. co. Stafford. 16. X. A Fatherless and Friendless.
(*b*) Henry Tragany. London. Merchant.
(*c*) Mariland. 7. Brothers Adventure. Capt. Henry Tragany.
(*d*) 12th. June 1684. Tho. Patteson. (Abra. Bayly. W. Smyth.) his father & mother & All friends dead & he a miserable wandering boy.

(*a*) D.615. Henry Snellgrove son of John Snelgrove. Everseft. co. Dorsett. 21. X.
(*b*) John Bright. London. Merchant.
(*c*) Virginia. 4. Booth. Capt. Peter Pagan.
(*d*) 28th. June 1684. Wm. Hunt. (Abra. Bayly.)

(*a*) D.616. John Mather son of John Mather decd. Ratley. co. Lancaster. Husbandman. 22. X.
(*b*) Wm. Haveland. London. Merchant.

(c) Barbadoes. 4. To serve as a Husbandman. Prince. Capt. Jonathan Wilson.
(d) 30th. June 1684. Tho. Patterson. (Abra. Bayly.)

(a) D.617. George Rook. Labourer. Cowcrosse. co. Middx. 21. X. Son of William Rook decd.
(b) John Johnson. London. Merchant.
(c) Barbadoes. To serve as a Labourer. Prince. Capt. Jonathan Wilson.
(d) 30th. June 1684. (no witness) (Abra. Bayly.)

(a) A.618. Richard Humphrys. 21. Signs.
(b) Richard Bayly of Maryland. Boatwright.
(c) Maryland. 4.
(d) 2nd, July 1684. Mark of William Sykes. (Abra. Bayly.)

(a) D.619. John Wright son of Wm. Wright. Markington (?). co. York. Groom. 23. X.
(b) Francis Parties. London. Merchant.
(c) Mariland. 4. To serve as a Groom. Benedict Leonard. Capt. Francis Parties.
(d) 2nd. July 1684. (no witness) (Abra. Bayly.)

(a) D.620. James Gresham son of James Gresham. Canterbury. co. Kent. 21. Groom. X.
(b) John Bright. London. Merchant.
(c) Virginia. 4. To serve as a Groom. Booth. Capt. Peter Pagan.
(d) 4th. July 1684. James Williams. (Abra. Bayly.)

(a) A.621. James Davis. 22. X.
(b) John Brown. London. Merchant.
(c) Virginia. 4.
(d) 4th. July 1684. Mark of Edmond Buckland. (Abra. Bayly.)

(a) D.622. William Harrex son of Ralph Harrex decd. Warrington. co. Lancaster. Cooper. 23. Signs.
(b) James Whaley. London. Merchant.
(c) Antego. 4. To serve as a Cooper. (no ship's name) Capt. Bowman.
(d) 4. July 1684. William beale. (Abra. Bayly.)

(a) D.623. Sarah Carter daughter of John Carter decd. Spinster. 19. X. NewCastle under Line. co. Staffs.
(b) Francis Parties. London. Merchant.
(c) Mariland. 4. Benedict Leonard. Capt. Francis Parties.
(d) 4th. July 1684. Wm. Howe. (Abra. Bayly. Ro: Hastings.)

(a) A.624. Elizabeth Bever. 21. X.
(b) John Wilkey. London. Marriner.
(c) Maryland. 4.
(d) 4th. July 1684. William Jones. (Abra. Bayly.)

(*a*) A.625. Margrett Weller. 22. Signs.
(*b*) Nicholas Smyth. Ratclif. Marriner.
(*c*) Maryland. 5.
(*d*) 4th. July 1684. Mark of Edward Dugles. (Abra. Bayly.)

(*a*) A.626. Thomas Lankford. 20. X. (Also called Lanford.)
(*b*) Perigrine Browne of London.
(*c*) Maryland. 6.
(*d*) 1st. July 1684. (Abra. Bayly. Ro: Hastings.)

(*a*) D.627. Joseph Johnson. About 22. From London. Son of Joseph Johnson. To be concerned a Slooper. Signs.
(*b*) Francis Parties. London. Merchant.
(*c*) Mariland. 4. To serve as a Sloper. Benedick Father. Capt. Francis Parties.
(*d*) 5th. July 1684. Edmund Puttman. (Abra. Bayly.)

(*a*) A.628. Bartholomew Stoell. A Husbandman. About 21. From Alborough, Surrey. Son of George Stowell. X.
(*b*) John Bright. London. Merchant.
(*c*) Virginia. 4. To serve as a Husbandman. Booth. Capt. Peter Pagan.
(*d*) 7th. July 1684. Joseph Pycraft. (Abra. Bayly.)

(*a*) D.629. Tho: Johnson. Labourer. Son of Ralph Johnson. From Portsmouth, co. Southton. About 19. Signs Thomas Johnson.
(*b*) John Bright. London. Merchant.
(*c*) Virginia. 4. Booth. Capt. Peter Pagan.
(*d*) 8th. July 1688 (sic, error for 1684). Tho: Wing (?). (Abra. Bayly. Ro: Hastings.)

(*a*) D.630. John Morrall. Gardner. About 22. From Newcastle-under-Line, co. Stafford. Son of Wm. Morrall. Signs.
(*b*) Edward Talbott. London. Merchant.
(*c*) Mariland. 4. To serve as a Gardner. Adventure. Capt. Ralph Cooper.
(*d*) 9th. July 1684. Edmund Pattinan. John Caller (?) (Abra. Bayly.)

(*a*) A.631. Jno. Hall. 21. Signs.
(*b*) Jno. Dicks. London.
(*c*) Maryland. 4.
(*d*) 9th. July 1684. Rich: Mosse. (Abra. Bayly.)

(*a*) A.632. William Fidler. 22. X.
(*b*) Captain John Brown. London. Marriner.
(*c*) Maryland. 4.
(*d*) 9th. July 1684. William Beale. (Abra. Bayly.)

(*a*) A.633. Robert Wright. 21. Signs.
(*b*) Captain John Brown. London. Marriner.
(*c*) Maryland. 4.
(*d*) 9th. July 1684. William Beale. (Abra. Bayly.)

(*a*) D.634. Andrew Oswald. A clerk. About 22. From Edenborough, Kingdom of Scotland. Son of James Oswald. Signs.
(*b*) John Bright. London. Merchant.
(*c*) Virginia. 4. Booth. Capt. Peter Pagan. £5 with him.
(*d*) 10th. July 1684. Edmo. Pattman. John Persea (?) (Abra. Bayly.)

(*a*) D.635. Thomas Lewis. A Gardner. About 22. From Peter Church, co. Hereford. Son of Thomas Lewis, deceased. Signs.
(*b*) John Bright. London. Merchant.
(*c*) Virginia. 4. To serve as a Gardner. Booth. Capt. Peter Pagan.
(*d*) 11th. July 1684. Tho. Pattman. (Abra. Bayly.)

(*a*) D.636. Elizabeth Johnson. Daughter of John Johnson from Sevenoaks, Kent. 21. Spinster. X.
(*b*) John Bright. London. Merchant.
(*c*) Virginia. 4. Booth. Capt. Peter Pagan.
(*d*) 14th. July 1684. Wm. Jones. (Abra. Bayly.)

(*a*) D.637. Robert Peal. Son of Daniell Peal. Groom. From Montsilly, co. Suffolk. 23. X.
(*b*) John Bright. London. Merchant.
(*c*) Virginia. 4. Booth. Capt. Peter Pagan.
(*d*) 14th. July 1684. Edmund Pattman. John Cabley. (Abra. Bayly.)

(*a*) A.638. Edward Holt. 22. Signs.
(*b*) John Perce (?) Limehouse. Mariner.
(*c*) Maryland. 4.
(*d*) 14th. July 1684. William Beale. (Abra. Bayly.)

(*a*) D.639. Phillipp Hide. A Taylor. 21. From Hereford, in county of the same. Son of Andrew Hide. X.
(*b*) John Bright. London. Merchant.
(*c*) Virginia. 4. To serve as a Tailor. Booth. Capt. Peter Pagan.
(*d*) 15th. July 1684. John Ashby X his mark. (Abra. Bayly.)

(*a*) A.640. An. Dowly. 25. X.
(*b*) Peter Peggin. London. Merchant.
(*c*) Maryland. 4.
(*d*) 15th. July 1684. Thomas Parkines. (Abra. Bayly.)

(*a*) A.641. Will: Hardin. 24. X.
(*b*) Richard Mosse. Mariner.
(*c*) Mariland. 4.
(*d*) 16th. July 1684. William Beale. (Abra. Bayly.)

(*a*) A.642. Elizabeth Lynes. 25.
(*b*) Isaack Lyon. Rotherhithe. Mariner.
(*c*) Maryland. 4.
(*d*) 16th. July 1684. Mark of X Thomas Cooper. (Abra. Bayly.)

(*a*) D.643. Robert Clapshoe. Son of Robert Clapshoe. From Newbury, co. Berks. A Woolcomer. About 22. X.
(*b*) Edward Burford. London. Merchant.
(*c*) Mariland. 4. To serve as a Woolcomer if their used. Abraham & Francis. Capt. Edward Burford.
(*d*) 16th. July 1684. James Williams. Tho. Puttiman. (Abra. Bayly.)

(*a*) A.644. Sarah Troke (?). 18. X.
(*b*) John Dix. London. Marriner.
(*c*) Maryland. 4.
(*d*) 17th. July 1684. Charles Bonman X his mark. (Abra. Bayly. Ro: Hastings.)

(*a*) D.645. Hannah Kible. About 21. From the parish and place of Etherson, co. Stafford. Daughter of John Kible. Spinster. X.
(*b*) Francis Parties. London. Merchant.
(*c*) Mariland. 4. Benedict Leonard. Capt. Francis Parties.
(*d*) 17th. July 1684. Wm. Cooper (?) (Abra. Bayly.)

(*a*) D.646. Wm. Harris. Son of Wm. Harris. From Alcham, co. Salop. 23. A Groom. X.
(*b*) Francis Parties. London. Merchant.
(*c*) Mariland. 4. To serve as a Groom. Benedict Leonard. Capt. Francis Parties.
(*d*) 17th. July 1684. Joseph Pycraft (?) Richard Waring. (Abra. Bayly.)

(*a*) D.647. Wm. Standley. Son of Wm. Standley. From Kingston-upon-Thames, co. Surrey. 22. A Cordwayner. Signs.
(*b*) Francis Parties. London. Merchant.
(*c*) Mariland. 4. To serve as a Cordwayner. Benedict Leonard. Capt. Francis Parties.
(*d*) 17th. July 1684. John Williams. (Abra. Bayly.)

(*a*) D.648. Wm. Cannaby (?) Son of John Cannaby (?) From Barkwell, co. Somerset. A Husbandman. 20. X.
(*b*) Francis Parties. London. Merchant.

52

(c) Mariland. 4. To serve as a Husbandman. Benedict Leonard. Capt. Francis Parties.
(d) 18th. July 1684. Richd. Parkines. (Abra. Bayly.)

(a) D.649. John Griggs. Son of Timothy Griggs. From St. Clements, co. Suffolk. 16. X.
(b) Francis Parties. London. Merchant.
(c) Mariland. 7. Benedict Leonard. Capt. Francis Parties.
(d) 18th. July 1684. Edmo. Patteman. (Abra. Bayly. Ro: Hastings.)

(a) D.650. John Morrey. Son of Robert Morrey. From St. Alhalloes, co. Northumberland. 21. A Labourer. Signs.
(b) John Haselwood. London. Merchant.
(c) Mariland. 4. To serve as a Labourer. Golden Lyon. Capt. Longman.
(d) 19th. July 1684. (No witness.) (Abra. Bayly.)

(a) D.651. Robert Scott. Son of Humphry Scott. From Nedheath (?), co. Salop. X.
(b) John Haslewood. London. Merchant.
(c) Mariland. 5. Golden Lyon. Capt. Longman.
(d) 19th. July 1684. Tho. Sympkins. (Abra. Bayly. Ro: Hastings.)

(a) D.652. John Cruse. Son of Thomas Cruse. From Plymton, co. Devon. About 21. A Cooper. Signs.
(b) Richard Batts. London. Merchant.
(c) Barbadoes. 4. To serve as a Cooper.
(d) 19th. July 1684. (No witness.) (Abra. Bayly.)

(a) A.653. Rich. Coles. 20. Signs.
(b) Rich. Mosse. Merchant.
(c) Mariland. 4.
(d) 21st. July 1684. Richard Howard X his mark. (Abra. Bayly. Ro: Hastings.)

(a) D.654. Mathew Morton. Son of Zachariah Morton. From Brintwood, co. Essex. 20. A friendless person. X.
(b) John Haselwood. London. Merchant.
(c) Mariland. 5. Golden Lyon. Capt. Longman.
(d) 21st. July 1684. John Williams. (Abra. Bayly. Ro: Hastings.)

(a) A.655. Thomas Kimberly. 21.
(b) John Dix. London. Marriner.
(c) Mariland. 4.
(d) 21st. July 1684. Charles Newnam. (Abra. Bayly.)

(a) D.656. John Dunbarr. A Taylor. About 22. Son of John Dunbarr. From Scotland, Glascow. Signs.

53

(*b*) Francis Parties. London. Merchant.
(*c*) Mariland. 4. To serve as a Taylor. Benedict Leonard. Capt. Francis Parties.
(*d*) 21st. July 1684. John Allexander. (Abra. Bayly.)

(*a*) D.657. Hugh Price (?) Son of Thomas Price (?) From Glasborough, co. Brecknockshire. 21. X.
(*b*) Francis Parties. London. Merchant.
(*c*) Mariland. 4. Benedict Leonard. Capt. Francis Parties.
(*d*) 22nd. July 1684. John Williams. Richard Waring. William Goodbourn. (Abra. Bayly.)

(*a*) D.658. Elizabeth Hanworth. Daughter of James Hanworth. From Goldston (?) co. Surrey. 27. Spinster. X.
(*b*) Edward Burford.
(*c*) Mariland. 4. Abraham & Francis. Capt. Edward Burford.
(*d*) 22nd. July 1684. John Ashley. (Abra. Bayly.)

(*a*) D.659. Daniell Francis. Son of Wm. Francis. From Shantly (?) co. Essex. 26. A Slooper. Signs.
(*b*) Francis Parties. London. Merchant.
(*c*) Mariland. 4. To serve as a Slooper. Benedict Leonard. Capt. Francis Parties.
(*d*) 22nd. July 1684. Joseph Pycroft. (Abra. Bayly.)

(*a*) A.660. Susan Clark. 20. X.
(*b*) Nicholas Smyth of London. Marriner.
(*c*) Maryland. 5.
(*d*) 23rd. July 1684. Ruben Cleeves. John Gand. (Abra. Bayly. Ro: Hastings.)

(*a*) D.661. Mary Jenkins. About 23. From parish or place of Wapping, co. Middx. Daughter of Wm. Jenkins. Spinster. X.
(*b*) Francis Parties of London. Merchant.
(*c*) Mariland. 4. Benedict Leonard. Capt. Francis Parties.
(*d*) 23rd. July 1684. John Harlie (?) John Rickards. (Abra-Bayly.)

(*a*) D.662. Timothy Clarkson son of John Clarkson from Cork. won (?), co. Lancaster. About 21. A Grome. Signs.
(*b*) Edward Burford of London. Merchant.
(*c*) Mariland. 4. To serve as a Grome. Abraham & Francis. Capt. Edward Burford.
(*d*) 23rd. July 1684. Joseph Pycraft. (Abra. Bayly.)

(*a*) D.663. Amy Hawes. Daughter of Robert Hawes from Titrill (?), co. Norfolk. 21. Spinster. X.
(*b*) Edward Burford of London. Merchant.
(*c*) Mariland. 4. Abraham & Francis. Capt. Edward Burford.
(*d*) 25th. July 1684. Richard Chesshire. Henry Justice. (Abra. Bayly.)

(*a*) A.664. William Sanders. 21. Signs.
(*b*) Capt. Phineas Hide.
(*c*) Maryland. 4.
(*d*) 26th. July 1684. William Daniell. (Abra. Bayly.)

(*a*) D.665. Wm. Taggwell, son of John Taggwell of Cleere (?), Wilts. Friendless person. 17. X.
(*b*) Francis Parties of London. Merchant.
(*c*) Mariland. 7. Benedict Leonard. Capt. Francis Parties.
(*d*) – July, 1684. Tho. Wood. (Abra. Bayly. Ro: Hastings.)

(*a*) D.666. Thomas Dalby son of John Dalby of Hainsley in co. Hereford. Gardner. 21. X.
(*b*) John Hazelwood of London. Merchant.
(*c*) Mariland. 4. Golden Lyon. Capt. Longman.
(*d*) 28th. July 1684. John Person. (Abra. Bayly.)

(*a*) D.667. Edward Phillips son of Thomas Phillips of Oulton (?) in co. Hereford. 21. Signs.
(*b*) Edward Burford of London. Merchant.
(*c*) Mariland. 4. Abraham and Francis. Capt. Edward Burford.
(*d*) 28th. July 1684. (No witness) (Abra. Bayly.)

(*a*) A.668. John Igne. 24. X.
(*b*) James Longman of Ratclif. Mariner.
(*c*) Virginia. 4.
(*d*) 28th. July 1684. William Beale. Bob. Stinsoone. (Abra. Bayly.)

(*a*) D.669. Thomas Hutton son of Thomas Hutton of Preston Parish, Scotland. 21. Slooper. Signs.
(*b*) John Haselwood of London. Merchant.
(*c*) Mariland. 4. Golden Lyon. Capt. Longman.
(*d*) 28th. July 1684. John Allexander (?). (Abra. Bayly.)

(*a*) D.670. Robert Seafield son of John Seafield of Hodgesdone, Midx. A poor youth. 16. X.
(*b*) Edward Talbott of London. Merchant.
(*c*) Mariland. 8. Crowne Malage (?) Capt. Staples.
(*d*) 11th. July 1684. Joseph Pycraft. (Abra. Bayly. Ro: Hastings.)

(*a*) A.671. Thomas Wakefield son of John and Mary Wakefield deceased. Signs.
(*b*) Richard Moss of London. Merchant.
(*c*) Maryland. 5.
(*d*) 28th. July 1684. John Williams. (Abra. Bayly. Ro: Hastings.)

(*a*) D.672. Anthony Stratford son of Charles Stratford of Tuiskbury (? Tewkesbury), Gloucester. Accomptant. Signs.
(*b*) John Hazelwood of London. Merchant.
(*c*) Mariland. 4. Golden Lyon. Capt. Longman.
(*d*) 28th. July 1684. John Person. (Abra. Bayly. Ro: Hastings.)

(*a*) A.673. John Johnson. 15. X.
(*b*) Richard Moss of London. Merchant.
(*c*) Maryland. 9.
(*d*) 28th. July 1684. John Dicks. (Abra. Bayly. Ro: Hastings.)

(*a*) A.674. William Evans. 17. X.
(*b*) Edward Burford of Virginia. Planter.
(*c*) Virginia. 5.
(*d*) 30th. July 1684. Henry Gedget. (Abra. Bayly. Ro: Hastings.)

(*a*) D.675. George Key. A shoemaker. Aged about 21 of B ... (?) in Lancaster. Son of Richard. X.
(*b*) Edward Burford of London. Merchant.
(*c*) Mariland. – Abraham and Francis. Capt. Edward Burford.
(*d*) 30th. July 1684. John Richards. (Abra. Bayly.)

(*a*) D.676. Nicholas Sharp. Accomptant. 22. Of Mayfield, Suffolk. Son of Nicholas. Signs.
(*b*) John Bright of London. Merchant.
(*c*) Mariland. 4. Booth. Capt. Peter Pagan.
(*d*) 30th. July 1684. John Person. Edmund Pittman. (Abra. Bayly.)

(*a*) D.677. Richard Baystow. Son of Wm. Baystow, deceased, of Parshin (?), Worcs. 21. Taylor. X.
(*b*) Edward Burford of London. Merchant.
(*c*) Mariland. 4. Abraham and Francis. Capt. Edward Burford.
(*d*) 30th. July, 1684. Robert Williamson. (Abra. Bayly.)

(*a*) D.678. William Ward. Husbandman. 21. Of Areton Hill, Kent. Son of Wm. Ward, deceased. Signs.
(*b*) John James of London. Merchant.
(*c*) Mariland. 4. Golden Lyon. Capt. Longman.
(*d*) 31st. July 1684. John Cooke. (Abra. Bayly.)

(*a*) D.679. John Harris, of Criplegate, Middlesex. Son of John Harris. 22. Signs.
(*b*) John Bright of London. Merchant.
(*c*) Virginia. 4. Booth. Capt. Peter Pagan.
(*d*) 31st. July 1684. Richard Wairing. (Abra. Bayly.)

(*a*) A.680. Jonathan Ward. 30. X.
(*b*) Richard Moss of London. Merchant.
(*c*) Maryland. 4.
(*d*) 31st. July 1684. William Beale. (Abra. Bayly.)

(*a*) 681. (A special form.) Mary Gibbs. Spinster. X.
(*b*) James Kendall. Mariner.
(*c*) Island of Jamaica. 4.

(d) 1st. August 1684. Thomas Gibbs. John Brasier. (Abra. Bayly. Ro: Hastings.)

This form is endorsed on the back as follows:—
Memo. that on the – day of Augt. 1684 Came and Appeared Before us ―― (left blank) Knts. & Aldermen of the Citty of London And two of his Majesties Justices of ye Peace of the sd. Citty Thomas Gibbs Cittizen and Leatherseller of London by trade a weaver And declared that Mary Gibbs the servant and Apprentice within named was lawfully bound to James Kendall within named according to ye Termes of ye Indenture within menconed By and with his acknowledge & free Consent And that he and the sd. Mary Gibbs & her freinds doe all approve hereof.

(a) A.682. Thomas Holtham. 19. Signs.
(b) Robert Hall of London. Marriner.
(c) Maryland. 5.
(d) 1st. August 1684. William Beale. (Abra. Bayly. Ro: Hastings.)

(a) A.683. Dinah Wells. 21. X.
(b) Edward Corbett of London. Mariner.
(c) In Virginia. 5.
(d) 1st. August 1684. William Beale. (Abra. Bayly.)

(a) D.684. Henry Willis, a Labourer. About 21. From Wantage, co. Berks. Son of Lenard Willis. X.
(b) John Moore of London. Merchant.
(c) Mariland. 4. John and Elizabeth. Capt. Kenzar.
(d) 1st. August 1684. (No witness.) (Abra. Bayly.)

(a) A.685. George Croson. 21. X.
(b) Edward Corbet of London. Marriner.
(c) In Virginia. 4.
(d) 1st. August 1684. William Beale. (Abra. Bayly.)

(a) A.686. Jeffery Badger. 29. X.
(b) Richard Batt of London. Merchant.
(c) In Maryland. 4.
(d) 1st. August 1684. William Beale. (Abra. Bayly.)

(a) A.687. Dorothy Jennings. About 21. X.
(b) Edward Corbet of London. Mariner.
(c) In Virginia. 5.
(d) 1st. August 1684. William Beale. (Abra. Bayly.)

(a) D.688. Elizabeth Liptrapp (?). Spinster. Daughter of Edward Liptrapp (?). About 21. X. From Tinbly, co. Leicester.
(b) John Moore of London. Merchant.

(*c*) Mariland. 4.
(*d*) 2nd. August 1684. Wm. Benson. Samuell Barker. (Abra. Bayly.)

(*a*) D.689. Thomas Haines. A Comemaker. Son of Stephen Haines. About 21. From London, co. Middx. X.
(*b*) John James of London. Merchant.
(*c*) Mariland. 4. Golden Lyon. Capt. Longman.
(*d*) 2nd. August 1684. Nath: Randell. Tho: Inn. (Abra. Bayly.) 20£ with him.

(*a*) D.690. Henry Wood. A Labourer. About 20. Son of Henry Wood, deceased. From Eastsmithfield, Middx. Signs.
(*b*) Edward Burford of London. Merchant.
(*c*) Meriland. 4. Abraham & Francis. Capt. Edward Burford.
(*d*) 4th. August 1684. Beniamin Johnson. (Abra. Bayly. Ro: Hastings.)

(*a*) A.691. Ellinor Draper. X.
(*b*) Richard Swanwell of New Castle. Marriner.
(*c*) Maryland in Virginnia. 4.
(*d*) 4th. August 1684. Laure. Wise . . . (?). (Abra. Bayly.)

(*a*) A.692. Ursula Child. 25. X.
(*b*) Richard Moss.
(*c*) Maryland. 4.
(*d*) 4th. August 1684. (No witnesses.) (Abra. Bayly.)

(*a*) A.693. John Bond. 23. Signs.
(*b*) Edmond Sandiford, of Barbadoes. Planter.
(*c*) Barbadoes. 4.
(*d*) 5th. August 1684. X mark of John Williams. (Abra. Bayly.)

(*a*) D.694. Jeremy Arnolld. A weaver. 22. Son of Thomas Honor (*sic*) deceased. From Coventry, co. Warwick. Signs ' Jeremiah Arnold '.
(*b*) Edward Burford of London. Merchant.
(*c*) Mariland. 4. Abraham & Francis. Capt. Edward Burford.
(*d*) 1st. August 1684. William goodbourne. (Abra. Bayly.)

(*a*) D.695. Frances Speakman. Spinster. 16. Daughter of George Speakman from Uxbridge in the County of Middx. deceased. X.
(*b*) John Moore of London. Merchant.
(*c*) Mariland. 4. Elizabeth & Katherine. Capt. Keazar.
(*d*) 5th. August 1684. Tho: Hutchens. (Abra: Bayly. Ro: Hastings.)

(*a*) A.696. Joseph Boreman. 22. X.
(*b*) Richard Moss of London. Merchant.

(c) Maryland. 5.
(d) 6th. August 1684. William Beale. (Abra. Bayly.)

(a) A.697. Mary Wood. 21. X.
(b) John Potter of Old Gravel Lane. Marriner.
(c) Maryland. 5.
(d) 6th. August 1684. Richd. Parkines. (Abra. Bayly.)

(a) D.698. Richard Eaststopp, by the consent of his friends. 16 From Petticoate Lane in Stepney Parish in co. Middx. Son of John Eastopp (*sic*) deceased. X.
(b) Thomas Rogers of London. Merchant.
(c) Mariland. 5. Loyall Subject. Capt. Thomas Rogers.
(d) 6th. August 1684. Precilla Eaton X her mark. Grandmother. Rich. Eaton the uncle. (Abra. Bayly. Ro: Hastings.)

(a) (A special form) 699. James Riggs. 22. Signs.
(b) Thomas Tench of London. Merchant.
(c) Maryland. 4.
(d) 6th. August 1684. X mark of Thomas Barrisford. (Abra. Bayly.)

(a) A.700. Robert Williams. 30. Signs Robt. Williams.
(b) Georg Green of London. Marriner.
(c) Virginia. 4.
(d) 7th. August 1684. John Barkeley. (Abra. Bayly.)

(a) A.701. William Freman. 18. X.
(b) Richd. Mosse. Merchant.
(c) Mariland. 7.
(d) 1st. August 1684. X mark of Edward Smith. (Abra. Bayly. Ro: Hastings.)

(a) D.702. John Smart. A taylor. 21. Son of John Smart, deceased, from Midlton co. Warwick. Signs.
(b) John Moore of London. Merchant.
(c) Mariland. 4. To serve as a taylor. Elizabeth & Katherine. Capt. Keazar.
(d) 7th. August 1684. Thomas Price. Abrahm Harris. (Abra. Bayly.)

(a) A.703. James Bankes. 18. X.
(b) Robert Hall of London. Marriner.
(c) Maryland. 6.
(d) 7th. August 1684. William Beale. (Abra. Bayly. Ro: Hastings.)

(a) A.704. Elinor Marchbanck. 22. X.
(b) Thomas Bradshaw of London. Marriner.
(c) Maryland. 5.
(d) 7th. August 1684. William Beale. (Abra. Bayly.)

(*a*) A.705. Henry Ingram. 16. X.
(*b*) Richard Moss.
(*c*) Maryland. 4.
(*d*) 7th. August 1684. X mark of Peter Howard. (Abra. Bayly. Ro: Hastings.)

(*a*) A.706. Luke Allyn. 18. X.
(*b*) John Twitt of London. Marriner.
(*c*) Maryland. 7.
(*d*) 7th. August 1684. William Beale. (Abra. Bayly. Ro: Hastings.)

(*a*) A special form. As No. 469. 707. Elizabeth Jones. Widdow. 26. Signs Eliz. Jones.
(*b*) James Kendall of Wappen. Commander of ye Ship called ye Hannah, now bound for Jamaica.
(*c*) Isle of Jamaica. 4. To be paid one shilling at the end of the Term.
(*d*) 8th. August 1684. Samll. Richardson. John Braside. John Bulkley. (Abra. Bayly.)

(*a*) (As No. 707) 708. Robbert Cros. 17. X.
(*b*) James Kendall.
(*c*) Island of Jamaica. 4. To be paid one shilling at the end of the Term.
(*d*) 8th. August 1684. X mark of Elesebeth Howard. X mark of Lawrence Howard. Eliz. Jones. (Abra. Bayly. Ro: Hastings.)

(*a*) (As No. 707) 709. Elizabeth Watts. 19. X.
(*b*) Thomas Tench.
(*c*) Maryland. 4.
(*d*) 9th. August 1684. Law. Wise Snr. (?). (Abra. Bayly. Ro: Hastings.)

(*a*) A.710. Jno. Boytor. 24. gorwider (? Gardener). X.
(*b*) Richd. Mosse. Merchant.
(*c*) Mariland. 4.
(*d*) 9th. August 1684. William Goodbourn. (Abra. Bayly.)

(*a*) A.711. Mary Hewit " Who on oath saith her father and mother are dead ". 18. X.
(*b*) Richard Cook of London. Marriner.
(*c*) Virginia. 4.
(*d*) 9th. August 1684. Elizabeth Parkines. (Abra. Bayly. Ro: Hastings.)

(*a*) (As No. 707) 712. Elizabeth Williams. 20. X.
(*b*) Thomas Tench.
(*c*) Mariland. 4.
(*d*) 9th. August 1684. Lawr. Wise Snr. (?). (Abra. Bayly. Ro: Hastings.)

(a) (As No. 707) 713. Lawrence Howard. 30. X.
(b) James Kendall.
(c) Jamaco. 4. To be paid one shilling at the end of the Term.
(d) 9th. August 1684. Edm: Thorisby. Rich: Wells. (Abra. Bayly.)

(a) D.714. George Terrold. A Clerk. 23. From Boston, co. Lincoln. Son of Joseph Terrold.
(b) Edward Burford of London. Merchant.
(c) Mariland. 4. To be employed as a Clerk. Abraham & Francis. Capt. Edward Burford.
(d) 9th. August 1684. John Person. (Abra. Bayly.) £5 with him.

(a) A.715. Elizabeth Powell. " Who maketh oath she is two and twenty years old." Signs Elizbeth Powell.
(b) Thomas Cocking of London. Marriner.
(c) Virginia. 4.
(d) 11th. August 1684. X mark of Thomas Davis. (Abra. Bayly.)

(a) A.716. William Peckden. 21. X.
(b) Robert Arche of London. Merchant.
(c) Virginia. 4.
(d) 11th. August 1684. John Daniell. (Abra. Bayly.)

(a) D. 717. Tho. Williams. A Groome. 18. From Llangdah, co. Glomorgan. X. Son of Wm. Williams. Dead.
(b) Thomas Arnold of London. Merchant.
(c) Virginia. Jefferies. Capt. Thomas Arnold.
(d) 11th. August 1684. William Pe . . . kin (?). John Williams. (Abra. Bayly. Ro: Hastings.)

(a) D.718. Thomas Walker. " A fatherless youth aged about 17 years." From . . . co. York. Son of George Walker. Signs.
(b) Edward Talbott of London. Merchant.
(c) Mariland or Virginia. 7. Crowne Malage. Capt. Staples.
(d) 12th. August 1684. X mark of John Bowles. (Abra. Bayly. Ro: Hastings.)

(a) A.719. Sarah Searl. 20. X.
(b) Richard Moss of London. Merchant.
(c) Maryland. 4.
(d) 12th. August 1684. William Beale. (Abra. Bayly. Ro: Hastings.)

(a) D.720. John Winch. A Pastry Cook. 25. Son of Richard Winch from St. Pulchres in the City of London. (? St. Sepulchre) Signs.
(b) Thomas Arnall of London. Merchant.
(c) Virginia. 4. To work as a Pastry Cook. Jefferies. Capt. Thomas Arnall.
(d) 12th. August 1684. Tho: Hutchens. (Abra. Bayly.) £5 with him.

(*a*) A.721. Susan Wharton. 21. X.
(*b*) Richard Moss of London. Merchant.
(*c*) Maryland. 4.
(*d*) 12th. August 1684. William Beale. (Abra. Bayly.)

(*a*) A.722. Mary Michell. 21. X.
(*b*) Richard Moss of London. Merchant.
(*c*) Maryland. 4.
(*d*) 12th. August 1684. William Beale. (Abra. Bayly.)

(*a*) A.723. Robert Cheeseman. 21. Signs.
(*b*) Thomas Chamberlain of London. Marriner.
(*c*) Virginia. 4.
(*d*) 12th. August 1684. William Beale. (Abra. Bayly.)

(*a*) A.724. Margret Pilkington. 23. X.
(*b*) Richard Moss of London. Merchant.
(*c*) Maryland. 4.
(*d*) 13th. August 1684. Richd. Parkines. (Abra. Bayly.)

(*a*) D.725. John Wood. A Groome. 22. Son of John Wood, Dead. From Ambrylin (?), co. York. X.
(*b*) Thomas Arnall of London. Merchant.
(*c*) Virginia. (No period stated) Jefferies. Capt. Thomas Arnall.
(*d*) 13th. August 1684. Richard Waring. (Abra. Bayly.) £5 with him.

(*a*) A.726. Ralf Barrow. 23. X.
(*b*) Christopher Daniell of London. Marriner.
(*c*) Maryland. 4.
(*d*) 12th. August 1684. John Shore. (Abra. Bayly.)

(*a*) D.727. Susanna Perry. A Spinster. About 20. From Early, co. Stafford. Daughter of James Perry. X.
(*b*) Edward Talbott of London. Merchant.
(*c*) Mariland or Virginia. 4. Crowne Malago. Capt. . . .
(*d*) 13th. August 1684. Henry . . . erington (?). (Abra. Bayly. Ro: Hastings.)

(*a*) A.728. Mabell Tynn. 18. X.
(*b*) Richard Moss of London. Merchant.
(*c*) Maryland. 4.
(*d*) 15th. August 1684. X mark of Edward Smyth. (Abra. Bayly. Ro: Hastings.)

(*a*) A.729. Edmond Ward. 23. X.
(*b*) Richard Moss. Merchant.
(*c*) Mariland. 4.
(*d*) 15th. August 1684. X mark of Thomas Berrisford.

(*a*) D.730. Ralfe Horsey. A Labourer. 25. Son of Phillipp Horsey. Born in Elminster, co. Summersett. X.

(*b*) John Moore of London. Merchant.
(*c*) Virginia. 4. To work as a Labourer. Assistance. Capt. James Strong.
(*d*) 15th. August 1684. John Rescorea (?). (Abra. Bayly.) 10*s*. with him.

(*a*) D.731. Wm. Hasteed. A Husbandman. 21. Son of Thomas Hasteed from Brosgrove, co. Sussex.
(*b*) John Bright of London. Merchant.
(*c*) Virginia. 4. Assistance. Capt. James Strong.
(*d*) 16th. August 1684. (No witness.) (Abra. Bayly.)

(*a*) A.732. Hannah Bowton. 30. X.
(*b*) Joseph Wosey of London. Merchant.
(*c*) Barbadoes. 4.
(*d*) 16th. August 1684. William Beale. (Abra. Bayly.)

(*a*) D.733. Anne Price. A Darimaid. About 22. From St. Andrews, co. Worcester. Daughter of John Price. Living. X.
(*b*) Edward Talbott of London. Merchant.
(*c*) Mariland. 4. To work as a Darimaid. Crowne Malago. Capt. Michael Stables.
(*d*) 16th. August 1684. (No witness.) (Abra. Bayly.)

(*a*) D.734. Thomas Weldon. Clerk. 21. Son of Thomas Weldon. Born in the town and Bishopprick of Durham. Signs.
(*b*) John Moore of London. Merchant.
(*c*) Virginia. 4. To work as a Clerk. Assistance. Capt. James Strong.
(*d*) 16th. August 1684. Tho. Winn (?). (Abra. Bayly.)

(*a*) D.735. Henry Lee. 18. X.
(*b*) John Moore of London. Merchant.
(*c*) Virginia. 5. Assistance. Capt. James Strong.
(*d*) 16th. August 1684. William Beale. (Abra. Bayly. Ro: Hastings.)

(*a*) D.736. William Dyer. A Labourer. 21. Son of George Dyer. Dead. From Martick, co. Summersett. X.
(*b*) Thomas Arnall of London. Merchant.
(*c*) Virginia. 5. Jefferies. Capt. Thomas Arnall.
(*d*) 16th. August 1684. Robt. Shankes. (Abra. Bayly.)

(*a*) D.737. Thomas Eavfens son of Lew. Eavfens. co. of Deaven. 18.
(*b*) John Bright of London. Merchant.
(*c*) Virginniah. 4. To work as a Husbandman. Assistance. Capt. James Strong.
(*d*) 16th. August 1684. (No witness.) (Abra. Bayly. Ro: Hastings.)

(*a*) D.738. George Herne. A Groom. 21. Son of George Herne from Woollinson, co. Gloucester.
(*b*) Thomas Arnall of London. Merchant.
(*c*) Virginia. 4. Jeffries. Capt. Thomas Arnall.
(*d*) 18th. August 1684. John Allward (?). (Abra. Bayly.)

(*a*) D.739. Richard Howes. A Husbandman. 21. Son of Wm. Howes. Dead. Born in Ossestrie, co. Salop. X.
(*b*) John Bright of London. Merchant.
(*c*) Virginia. 4. Assistance. Capt. James Strong.
(*d*) 18th. August 1684. Tho. Hertehouse (?). (Abra. Bayly.)

(*a*) A.740. Frances Banister. 21. X.
(*b*) John Twitt of London. Marriner.
(*c*) Maryland. 5.
(*d*) 18th. August 1684. William Beale. (Abra. Bayly.)

(*a*) D.741. John Beckett. Naylor. 24. From Bishoppbery (?) co. Stafford. Son of Tho. Beckett. Living. X.
(*b*) John Bright of London. Merchant.
(*c*) Virginia. 4. To work as a Naylor. Assistance. Capt. James Strong.
(*d*) 18th. August 1684. Edwd. Pat ... (?) Thos. W ... (?). (Abra. Bayly.)

(*a*) E.742. Mary Hutchins. 22. X.
(*b*) Frederick Johnson of London. Marriner.
(*c*) Maryland. 4.
(*d*) 15th. August 1684. X mark of Grace Gilbart. (Abra. Bayly.)

(*a*) E.743. Edward Macherness. 23. Signs "Edward Makerness".
(*b*) Andrew Peterson of Ratclif. Mariner.
(*c*) Virginia. 4.
(*d*) 19th. August 1684. William Beal. John Mills. (Abra. Bayly.)

(*a*) E.744. John Hill. 18. Signs.
(*b*) William Haveland of London. Marchant.
(*c*) Virginia. 5.
(*d*) 15th. August 1684. (No witness.) (Abra. Bayly. Ro: Hastings.)

(*a*) E.745. Thomas Naylor. 31. Signs.
(*b*) Thomas Arnold of London. Marriner.
(*c*) Virginia. 4.
(*d*) 19th. August 1684. William Beale. Walter Marshall. (Abra. Bayly.)

(*a*) A.746. Anderous Mattson, a Swead aged 18. Signs "Anders Mattzon".
(*b*) Christopher Prisick.
(*c*) In Barbadoes. 4.
(*d*) 31st. January 1683. Jon. Ingham. (Abra. Bayly.)

(*a*) B.747. Mathew Scott. From Scotland. 23. X.
(*b*) Christopher Prissick of London. Marriner.
(*c*) Barbadoes. 4. Barbadoes Merchant. Capt. Christopher Prissick.
(*d*) 6th. February 1683. Jon. Ingham. (Abra. Bayly.)

(*a*) B.748. Humphry Jones. Burnham, Essex. Son of Wm. Jones. dd. 19. Signs.
(*b*) Christopher Prissick, of London. Marriner.
(*c*) Barbadoes. 6. Barbadoes Merchant. Capt. Christopher Prissick.
(*d*) 8th. February 1683. Richard Waring. Tho: Patterson. (Abra. Bayly. Ro: Hastings.) Ye sd. Jones made oath yt. his father & mother was wiling to his goeinge.

(*a*) B.749. Joseph George. Leachfield, Stafford. Son of John George. 31. Signs.
(*b*) Christopher Prissick of London. Marriner.
(*c*) Barbadoes. (No term.) To be employed as a Tayler. Barbadoes Merchant. Capt. Christopher Prissick.
(*d*) 9th. February 1683. John Perse (?). (Abra. Bayly.)

(*a*) B.750. Pauls Cornelius. From Zealand in Holland. 18. X.
(*b*) Christopher Prissick of London. Marriner.
(*c*) Barbadoes. 5. Barbadoes Merchant. Capt. Christopher Prissick.
(*d*) 14th. February 1683. Jon. Ingham. (Abra. Bayly.)

(*a*) A.751. William Thomson. 12. X.
(*b*) John Humfrys of London. Marriner.
(*c*) Jamaca. 7.
(*d*) 18th. February 1683. (Abra. Bayly.) His own father who is willing to his going being examined by Oath. X mark of Richard Thomson ye father. William Langford.

(*a*) B.752. Wm. ffrost. Windham, Norfolk. Son of Edward ffrost. dd. 18. X.
(*b*) Christopher Pressick, of London. Marriner.
(*c*) Barbadoes. 7. Barbadoes Merchant. Capt. Christopher Pressick.
(*d*) 21st. February 1683. X mark of Edmund Puttmam. (Abra. Bayly. Ro: Hastings.)

(*a*) B.753. James Backwell. Middx. Cordwayner. 25. Signs.
(*b*) John Dix of London. Merchant.
(*c*) Barbadoes. 4. To work as a Cordwayner. Crowne. Capt. Croft.
(*d*) 27th. February 1683. (No witness.) (Abra. Bayly.)

(*a*) B.754. Michel Drumner. 21. X.
(*b*) John James of London. Merchant.
(*c*) Barbadoes. 4. Crowne. Capt. Croft.
(*d*) 29th. February 1683. Jon. Ingham. (Abra. Bayly.)

(*a*) A.755. George Trope. 21. Signs.
(*b*) John Dix.
(*c*) Barbadoes. 4. To be employed as a " Slicker " (?).
(*d*) 1st. March 1683. Jon. Ingham. (Abra. Bayly.)

(*a*) B.756. John Browne. Middx. Butcher. 33. Signs.
(*b*) John Brown of London. Merchant. (Note: This is an error for John Neale.)
(*c*) Jamaica. 4. To work as a Butcher. Providence. Capt. Bartholomew.
(*d*) 6th. March 1683. Jon. Ingham. (Abra. Bayly.)

(*a*) B.757. Henry Phelix. Middx. Cooper. 22 (?) X.
(*b*) John Earle of London. Merchant.
(*c*) Antegoe. 4. To work as a Cooper. Francis & Dorothy. Capt. Rich. Brigham.
(*d*) 7th. March 1683. Jon. Ingham. (Abra. Bayly.) £5 with him.

(*a*) B.758. Thomas Agersall. Middx. 20. X.
(*b*) John Earle of London. Marriner.
(*c*) Antego. 6. Francis & Dorothy. Capt. Richard Brigham.
(*d*) 7th. March 1683. Wm. Hastings. Examined and bound before us two of his Mats. Justices of the Peace for the County of Middx. the date afore written att the Sessions held for the Tower Division att Whitechapell Courthouse and the said Thomas Agersall was turned out of the house of Correction as a vagrant. (Abra. Bayly. Ro: Hastings.)

(*a*) B.759. Richard White. Middx. about 21. X.
(*b*) John Earle of London. Marriner.
(*c*) Antego. 4. Francis & Dorothy. Capt. Richard Brigham.
(*d*) 7th. March 1683. Wm. Hastings. Examined and bound before us two of his Mats. Justices of the Peace for the County of Middx. the date aforewritten at the Sessions held for the Tower Division att Whitechappell Court house and the said Richard White was turned out of the house of Correction as a Vagrant. (Abra. Bayly. Ro: Hastings.)

(*a*) B.760. Rich. Price. Middx. A Cooper. 23. Signs " Richard Price ".
(*b*) John Earle of London. Merchant.
(*c*) Jamaica. 4. To work as a Cooper. Joseph. Capt. John Brakes.
(*d*) 8th. March 1683. Tho. Guy Jnr. (Abr. Bayly.) This person came just out of Whitechapell prison for debt.

(*a*) B.761. Nicholas Browne. Middx. A Groome. 24. X.
(*b*) John Williams of London. Merchant.
(*c*) Antego. 4. Tc work as a Groome. Francis & Dorothy. Capt. Richd. Bridgman.
(*d*) 13th. March 1683. Jon. Ingham. (Abra. Bayly.)

(*a*) B.762. Daniel Maginn (or Macquin) of the Kingdom of Scotland. 21. X.
(*b*) John Rose of London. Merchant.
(*c*) Antego. 4. Francis & Dorothy. Capt. Bridgman.
(*d*) 15th. March 1683. (No witness.) (Abra. Bayly.)

(*a*) A.763. Mary May. 21. X.
(*b*) Samson Stoder.
(*c*) New England. 4.
(*d*) 15th. March 1683. Jon. Ingham. (Abra. Bayly.)

(*a*) B.764. John Smith. Middx. Brickmaker. 28. X.
(*b*) John Jones of London. Merchant.
(*c*) Jamaica. 4. To work as a Brickmaker. Providence. Capt. Bartholomew.
(*d*) 17th. March 1683. William Goodbourn. (Abra. Bayly.)

(*a*) B.765. Samuel Gent. County Warwick. 27. X.
(*b*) Richard Batts of London. Merchant.
(*c*) Jamaica. 4. Providence. Capt. Bartholomew.
(*d*) 18th. March 1683. Tho: Hutchens. (Abra. Bayly.)

(*a*) B.766. David Addamson of the Kingdom of Scotland. 23. X.
(*b*) John Williams of London. Merchant.
(*c*) Jamaica. 4. Providence. Capt. Bartholomew.
(*d*) 26th. March 1684. John Person. Richard Waring. (Abra. Bayly.)

(*a*) B.767. Robt. Pettenreck (?), of the Kingdom of Scotland. Accomptant. 21. Signs.
(*b*) Richard Batts of London. Merchant.
(*c*) Jamaica. 4. To serve as an Accomptant. George. Capt. Jones.
(*d*) 27th. March 1684. John Earle. (Abra. Bayly.)

(*a*) B.768. John Reed, of the Kingdom of Scotland. Groome. 21.
(*b*) Richard Batts of London. Merchant.
(*c*) Jamaica. 4. To serve as a Groome. George. Capt. Jones.
(*d*) 27th. March 1684. John Earle. (Abra. Bayly.)

(*a*) B.769. Thomas Frame (?). Middx. A Ploughman. 30. X.
(*b*) John Mason of London. Merchant.
(*c*) Antego. 4. To serve as a Ploughman. Francis & Dorothy. Capt. Richd. Bridgman.
(*d*) — March 1683. Charles Uphman. (Abra. Bayly.)

(a) A.770. James Almond. 11. X.
(b) Edmond Pain of Brook Street, in the parish of Stepney, Middx. Mariner.
(c) Marylande. 9.
(d) 4th. April 1684. Edward Bedford his father in law. John Beardmore his uncle. John Karford (?Harford) his uncle. Examined before me one of his Maties. Justices of peace for Middlesex in the presence of his father in law and two of his uncles who are witnesses hereto & consent, his own father & mother being dead. (Abra. Bayly.)

(a) B.771. Jonathan Miller. County of Northampton. 24. X.
(b) Edmund Pattman of London. Merchant.
(c) Antego. 4. Anne & Mary. Capt. Harry.
(d) 7th. April 1684. (No witness.) (Abra. Bayly.)

(a) B.772. William Braisnett. Hethersett, Norfolk. Labourer. 21. X.
(b) John Hill of London. Merchant.
(c) Antego. 4. To work as a Labourer. Anne & Mary. Capt. Isaack Harvey.
(d) 8th. April 1684. Tho: James. (Abra. Bayly.)

(a) A.773. Abraham Amis (or Anis). 31. X.
(b) Edmond Pain of London. Merchant.
(c) Pensilvania. 4.
(d) 9th. April 1684. Edmond Payne, Juner. (Abra. Bayly.)

(a) A.774. Joseph Vaughan. 33. Signs "Jos. Vaughan" in a good hand.
(b) Edmond Pain of London. Merchant.
(c) Maryland.
(d) 9th. April 1684. Edmond Payne, Juner. (Abra. Bayly.)

(a) B.775. Abell Crode. From Cutlock, Dorset. 26. X.
(b) Sr. Henry Johnson Knt. of London. Merchant.
(c) Carolena. 4. To work as a Husbandman. Joseph & Ashton, Capt, John Jones.
(d) 14th. April 1684. (No witness.) (Abra. Bayly.)

(a) B.776. Daniel Gardner. Berdly, Worcestershire. Labourer. 26. X.
(b) Sir Henry Johnson Knt. of London. Merchant.
(c) Carolena. 4. To work as a Labourer. Joseph & Ashton. Capt. John Jones.
(d) 14th. April 1684. Samuell Barker. (Abra. Bayly.)

(a) B.777. Alice Gardner. Beudly, Worcestershire. Spinster. 24. X.
(b) Sir Henry Johnson Knt. of London. Merchant.

(c) Carolena. 4. John (*sic*) & Ashton. Capt. John Jones.
(d) 14th. April 1684. Samuell Barker. (Abra. Bayly.)

(a) A.778. Stephen Williams. 31. X.
(b) Edward Padly of Popler. Marriner.
(c) Antegoe. 4.
(d) 17th. April 1684. Walter Preston. (Abra. Bayly.)

(a) B.779. John Hollis. From county Stafford. 24. X.
(b) John Hall of London. Merchant.
(c) Barbadoes. 4. John & Elizabeth. Capt. Jonas Leech.
(d) 22nd. April 1684. Richard Waring. (Abra. Bayly.)

(a) A780. Benjamen Phillips. 21. Signs " Benjamin Phillips ".
(b) John Jones of London. Mariner.
(c) Carolina. 4.
(d) 22nd. April 1684. John Ransom. (Abra. Bayly.)

(a) B.781. Abraham Taylor. Ashton under. (*sic*) co. Lancaster. 20. X.
(b) John Hall of London. Merchant.
(c) Barbadoes. 4. John & Elizabeth. Capt. Jonas Leech.
(d) 22nd. April 1684. Richard Waring. (Abra. Bayly.)

(a) B. 782. Martin Gardner, from Edenborough. 28. Signs.
(b) John Hall of London. Merchant.
(c) Barbadoes. 4. To serve as a Husbandman. John & Elizabeth. Capt. Jonas Linch. (*sic.* ? an error for Leech.)
(d) 22nd. April 1684. John Sh.... (?) (Abra. Bayly.)

(a) A.783. An Hill. 21. X.
(b) William Orton of Ratclif. Mariner.
(c) Virginia. 4.
(d) 24th. April 1684. David Carr. X the mark of Hosea (?) Cole her own sister who makes oath her father & mother are both dead. (Abra. Bayly.)

(a) B. 784. Henry Bisford from the Cittie & County of York. 28. X.
(b) George Smith of London. Merchant.
(c) Jamaica. 4. To serve as a Husbandman. Richard & Sarah. Capt. Thomas Stubbs.
(d) 25th. April 1684. James Williams. (Abra, Bayly.)

(a) B.785. Ffrancis Bromfield. co. Sussex. Farrier Smith. 24. X.
(b) William Haveland of London. Merchant.
(c) Barbadoes. 4. To serve as a Farrier Smith. John & Elizabeth. Capt. Jonas Leech.
(d) 26th. April 1684. John Cooke. (Abra. Bayly.)

(a) B.786. Wm. Harrison from Masson (? Masham) co. York. Taylor. 30. Signs.

(b) James Williams of London. Merchant.
(c) Barbadoes. 4. To serve as a Taylor. Ffriendship. Capt. Wm. Bedding.
(d) 30th. April 1684. John Cooke. (Abra. Bayly.)

(a) B.787. Edward Button from Atleborough co. Norfolk. Baker. 28. Signs.
(b) John Smith of London. Merchant.
(c) Jamaica. 4. To serve as a Baker. Richard & Sarah. Capt. Thomas Stubbs.
(d) 5th. May 1684. John Richards. (Abra. Bayly.)

(a) B.788. Robert Mercer from Lowding in the Kingdom of Scotland. Baker. 28. Signs " Robert Merser."
(b) John Smith of London. Merchant.
(c) Jamaica. 4. To serve as a Baker. Richard & Sarah. Capt. Thomas Stubbs.
(d) 6th. May 1684. John Richards. (Abra. Bayly.)

(a) A.789. Rebeccah Hill. 21. X.
(b) John Morehead of Jamaica. Merchant.
(c) Jamaica. 4.
(d) 10th. May 1684. Mark X of Lewis Reed. (Abra. Bayly.)

(a) A.790. Elizabeth Harris. X.
(b) James Philip of Plimoth. (i.e. Plymouth) Mariner.
(c) Virginia or Carolina. 4.
(d) 20th. May 1684. Mark X of Robert Standinott (?). (Abra. Bayly.)

(a) (A special printed form) 791. Ffrancis Stott. 28.
(b) William Smith of Wapping, Middx. Marriner.
(c) PenSilvania.
(d) 23rd. May 1684. Tho: Butler. (Abra. Bayly.)

(a) A.792. Charles Horton. 13. X.
(b) William pewsey of Tower Hill. Merchant.
(c) Jamaica. 9.
(d) 23rd. May 1684. Elias Bayley. (Examined before me a Justice of Peace for Middlesex in the presence of his own father William Horton who consents to his going. Abra. Bayly.)

(a) D.793. Thomas Lingwood. Son of Christopher Lingwood from High Easterne co. Essex. A Coachman. 27. Signs " Thomas Linggood."
(b) John Jones of London. Merchant.
(c) Barbadoes. 4. To serve as a Coachman. Ffriendship. Capt. Wm. Bedding.
(d) 25th. May 1694. John Williams. (Abra. Bayly.)

(a) D.794. John Harding. Son of John Harding deceased. From Poroth (?) co. Cumberland. 30. A Husbandman. X.
(b) William Haveland.
(c) Barbadoes. 4. To serve as a Husbandman. Ffriendship. Capt. William Bedding.
(d) 26. May 1684. Mark X of Edmund Patman. (Abra. Bayly.)

(a) A.795. Elizabeth Beman. 23. X.
(b) James Gallaway of Whitechappel. Marriner.
(c) Maryland. 4.
(d) 29th. May 1684. George Harmer. (Abra. Bayly.)

(a) D.796. John Lee, son of John Lee deceased. From Cillell, co. Warwick. 21. A Lock Smith. X.
(b) John Jones of London. Merchant.
(c) Barbadoes. 4. To serve as a Lock Smith. Ffriendship. Capt. Wm. Bedding.
(d) 31st. May 1684. Tho. Sympkiss. (?) (Abra. Bayly.)

(a) D.797. John Andrew. A Husbandman. Aged about 22. From Mawkcon (?) co. Hertford Son of John Andrew deceased Ploughman. X.
(b) William Haveland of London. Merchant.
(c) Barbadoes. 4. To serve as a Ploughman. Ffriendship. Capt. William Haveland. (*sic*).
(d) 2nd. June 1684. Mark X of George Hill. (Abra. Bayly.)

(a) A.798. Hannah Webb. 19. X.
(b) James Galwith of Stepny. Mariner.
(c) Mariland. 4.
(d) 2nd. June 1684. William Webb. Mark X of Hannah Booke(r) her own Aunt. (Examined in the presence of her own Father William Webb and her own Mother Consenting before me her being witness hereto. Abra. Bayly, a Justice of Peace for Middlesex.)

(a) D.799. Evan Price. A Husbandman. Aged about 21. Son of David Price. X. From Manavan (? Manafon), co. Montgomery.
(b) John Browne of London. Merchant.
(c) Jamaica. 4. To serve as a Husbandman. Wm. & Mary. Capt. Mingiam.
(d) 3rd. June 1684. John Person. (Abra. Bayly.)

(a) D.800. Richard Worrell. Son of Richard Worrell. From Great Budworth, co. Chester. Aged about 27. A Husbandman. X.
(b) John Browne of London. Merchant.
(c) Jamaica. 4. To serve as a Husbandman. Wm. & Mary. Capt. Mingiam.
(d) 3rd. June 1684. Perygreen Cooke. (Abra. Bayly.)

(*a*) D.801. Gabriel Ely. A Ploughman. Aged about 21. From Duffield, co. Derby. Son of George Ely deceased. X.
(*b*) John Browne of London. Merchant.
(*c*) Jamaica. 4. To serve as a Ploughman. Wm. & Mary. Capt. Mingiam.
(*d*) 3rd. June 1684. Mickel Scott. (Abra. Bayly.)

(*a*) A.802. John Moody. 22. Signs.
(*b*) Robert Lockton of Shadwell. Mariner.
(*c*) Jamaca. 4.
(*d*) 3rd. June 1684. Charles Bruice (?). (Abra. Bayly.)

(*a*) A.803. Elizabeth Piddock. 24. X.
(*b*) Nicholas Smyth of Ractlif. Marriner.
(*c*) Maryland. 5.
(*d*) 4th. June 1684. Mark X of Edward Duglos. (Abra. Bayly.)

(*a*) A.804. John Horton. 23. X.
(*b*) Rainsford Waterhows of London. Merchant.
(*c*) Jamaca. 4.
(*d*) 5th. June 1684. Tho. Larke. (Abra. Bayly.)

(*a*) A.805. Dockas Rawlett. 19. X.
(*b*) Nicholas Smyth of Ratcliff. Marriner.
(*c*) Maryland. 5.
(*d*) 5th. June 1684. John Rowlandson. Wm. Gosling. (Abra. Bayly.) Her father & mother dead & her Brother Charles (?) present at her binding.

(*a*) A.806. Robert Little (? Littler). 22. X.
(*b*) Ransford Waterhows of London. Merchant.
(*c*) Jamaca. 4.
(*d*) 7th. June 1684. Tho. Larke. (Abra. Bayly.)

(*a*) D.807. Christopher Desper. A Ploughman. Aged about 27.
(*b*)   From Goldas (?) co. Kent. Son of Henry Desper. X. John Browne of London. Merchant.
(*c*) Jamaica. (no term) To serve as a Ploughman. William & Mary. Capt. Mingiam.
(*d*) 7th. June 1684. John Cooke. (Abra. Bayly.)

(*a*) A.808. Susan Clark. 21. X.
(*b*) Robert Hassett of London. Merchant.
(*c*) Jamaca. 4.
(*d*) 9th. June 1684. Robert Loughte. (Abra. Bayly.)

(*a*) D.809. Wm. Downes son of John Downes from Tenbury co. Worcester. Aged about 27. X.
(*b*) Wm. Haveland of London. Merchant.

(c) Mariland. 4. To serve as a Husbandman.
(d) 9th. June 1684. Mark X of Edmund Puttman. (Abra. Bayly.)

(a) D.810. Andrew Breeding son of Thomas Breeding. 20. A Scotchman. X.
(b) Wm. Haveland of London. Merchant.
(c) Mariland. 4. Brothers Adventure. Capt. Henry Tragany.
(d) 10th. June 1684. John Rodgers. (Abra. Bayly.)

(a) A.811. William Bagott. 26. Signs.
(b) William Orton of Ratclif. Marriner.
(c) Carolina or Virginia. 4.
(d) 11th. June 1684. Henry Hall. (Abra. Bayly.)

(a) A.812. John Shelton. 18. Signs.
(b) David Car of London. Mariner.
(c) Carolina or Virginia. 4.
(d) 12th. June 1684. Richd. Parkines. (The said John Shelton made oath before me that his Mother is dead & his father knew & was willing to his going. Abra. Bayly.)

(a) A.813. Thomas Lucas. 30. X.
(b) David Carr of London. Mariner.
(c) Virginia or Carolina. 4.
(d) 12th. June 1684. Christopher Baylif. (Abra. Bayly.)

(a) D.814. Wm. Feaser son of Wm. Feaser from Ortnay (? Orkney) A Scotchman. Aged about 21. An Accomptant. Signs " William Fraser."
(b) Henry Tragany of London. Merchant.
(c) Mariland. 4. To serve as an Accomptant. Brothers Adventure. Capt. Henry Tragany.
(d) 12th. June 1684. John Shawe. (Abra. Bayly.)

(a) D.815. Marke Watts son of George Watts. From Furbright co. Surrey. Aged about 21. A Husbandman. X.
(b) Henry Tragany of London. Merchant.
(c) Mariland. 4. To serve as a Husbandman. Brothers Adventure Capt. Henry Tragany.
(d) 13th. June 1684. James Williams. (Abra. Bayly.)

(a) D.816. John Johnson son of John Johnson. From Liverpoole co. Lancaster. Aged about 29. Accomptant. Signs.
(b) John Browne of London. Merchant.
(c) Jamaca. 4. To serve as an Accomptant. William and Mary. Capt. Mingiam.
(d) 13th. June 1684. John Cooke. (Abra. Bayly.)

(a) D.817. John Pirkins from Tyverton co. Devon. Son of William Pirkins. Aged 28. A Husbandman. X.
(b) Henry Tragany of London. Merchant.

(*c*) Mariland. 4. To serve as a Husbandman. Brothers Adventure. Capt. Henry Tragany.
(*d*) 14th. June 1684. Joseph Parns. (Abra. Bayly.)

(*a*) D.818. Joseph Guy son of Wm. Guy from Westborough co. Wilts. Aged about 29. A Cordwayner. X.
(*b*) Henry Tragany of London. Merchant.
(*c*) Maryland. 4. To serve as a Cordwayner. Brothers Adventure. Capt. Henry Tragany.
(*d*) 16th. June 1684. Frances Williams. (Abra. Bayly.)

(*a*) D.819. Henry Chambers son of John Chambers from Holdernesse co. York. Aged about 30. A Schollar. Signs.
(*b*) Henry Tragany of London. Merchant.
(*c*) Mariland. 4. To serve as an Accomptant. Brothers Adventure. Capt. Henry Tragany.
(*d*) 16th. June 1684. (No witnesses.) (Abra. Bayly).

(*a*) D.820. Thomas Martin son of Gilbert Martin from Morpeth co. Cumberland. Aged about 16. X.
(*b*) Henry Tragany of London. Merchant.
(*c*) Maryland. 7. Brothers Adventure. Capt. Henry Tragany.
(*d*) 16th. June 1684. Richson (?) Pepper. His mark. (Abra. Bayly. John Berry.)
This boy's father and Mother wear both dead his father died abought eight years since and his Mother a bought six years in New Cassell whear he was kept at the Charg of ye parish & from thence came hether.

(*a*) D.821. John Haster son of John Haster from Edenborough, Scotland. Aged about 21. A Labourer. Signs.
(*b*) Henry Tragany of London. Merchant.
(*c*) Mariland. 4. To serve as a Labourer. Brothers Adventure. Capt. Henry Tragany.
(*d*) 17th. June 1684. Robert Williamson. (Abra. Bayly.)

(*a*) D.822. Wm. Farratt son of Wm. Farratt from Hartperer (?) co. Chester. Aged about 19. A fatherless and friendless. X.
(*b*) John Bright of London. Merchant.
(*c*) Virginia. 5. Booth. Capt. Peter Pagam.
(*d*) 18th. June 1684. John Crose. (John Berry. Abra. Bayly.)

(*a*) D.823. John Browne son of John Browne, by his consent. From Tillingham co, Essex. Aged about 18. Poore. X.
(*b*) John Bright of London. Merchant.
(*c*) Virginia. 5. Booth. Capt. Peter Pagam.
(*d*) 19th. June 1684. James Davis. Isaac Hartwell. (Abra. Bayly.)
This boy his father and Mother being both dead was desired by ye parish to be sent to sea. (Note the original Indenture

apprenticeing John Browne a poor child of the parish of Tillingham to Daniell Gardner, to be taught Seafareing and Drudging, dated 11th. July 1682, is attached.)

The following note is also attached :

Memorandum that whereas John Browne the son of John Brown of Tillingham in ye County of Essex was bound out an Apprentice upon July ye 11th. 1682 To Daniel Gardiner of St. Laurance in ye sd. County, It is now Agreed to by the said John Browne the Father and Daniel Gardiner The Master that the said John Browne the Younger shall bee at the service and disposal of James Dayves of Christchurch in Surrey And to bee by him and His Assignees fairly used And the said James Davyes is to discharge John Browne the Father and the Parish of Tillingham from him the sd. John Browne the younger for the space of five years to come from ye date hereof. Dated the 17th. Day of June 1684.

With the consent of us the Inhabitants of Tillingham whose names are underwritten.

Matthew Elliston. Vicar.
ffran: Metcalfe.
James Corbett.
William Church.
Ed: Elmes.

Ye Markes of

John   Browne Senior
X   X
Daniell.   Gardner.

(*a*) D.824. Symon Wilson. Son of Wm. Wilson from Kingham co. Oxon. A Cittizon & Merch. Taylor of London. Aged 31. Signs " Simon Willson ".
(*b*) William Thomas of London. Merchant.
(*c*) Barbadoes. 4. To serve as a Taylor. Prince. Capt. Jonathan Wilson.
(*d*) 23rd. June 1684. James Kinsman. (Abra. Bayly.)

(*a*) D.825. John ffitch son of John ffitch from Arringtown (?) co. Cambridge. Aged about 20. X
(*b*) John Bright of London. Merchant.
(*c*) Virginia. 4. Booth. Captain Peter Pagan.
(*d*) 24th. June 1684. John Williams. (Abra. Bayly. John Berry.)
     He made oath his father & Mother wear both dead & he not a Servant nor ever had been.

(*a*) A.826. Kathrine Gardner. 22. X.
(*b*) Georg Clark of London. Mariner.
(*c*) Carolina. 4.
(*d*) 26th. June 1684. Tho. Guy. (Abra. Bayly.)
     She was taken out of Bridewell after she had layn thear two months for pilfering.

(*a*) A.827. William Harrison. 31. Signs " Will. Harrison ".
(*b*) Thomas Everard of Limehows. Marriner.
(*c*) Barbadoes. 4.
(*d*) 26th. June 1684. William beale. (Abra Bayly.)

(*a*) A.828. Mary Dwaite. 21. X.
(*b*) Georg Clarq of London. Mariner.
(*c*) Carolina. 4.
(*d*) 26th. June 1684. Tho. Guy. (Abra. Bayly.)
She was taken out of Bridwell after she had layn thear two Months for pilfering.

(*a*) A.829. Samuell Lee. 18. X.
(*b*) Francis French of London. Merchant.
(*c*) Maryland. 6.
(*d*) 30th. June 1684. (Witness) his one Mother, his father being dead, who consented, taken out of Bridewell. Mark of Alice (?) Lee his Mother. Tho. Guy. (Abra. Bayly. W. Smyth.)

(*a*) A.830. Joseph Lee. 14. X.
(*b*) Francis French of London. Merchant.
(*c*) Maryland. 7.
(*d*) 30th. June 1684. (Witness) his one Mother, who consented, his father being dead, taken out of Bridewell. Tho. Guy. Mark of Alice (?) Lee the Mother. (Abra. Bayly. W. Smyth.)

(*a*) D.831. Wm. Lithemore, a Ploughman. Aged about 30. From Great Budworth (?) co. Chester. Son of Wm. Lithemore. X.
(*b*) John Browne of London. Merchant.
(*c*) Jamaica. 4. To serve as a Ploughman. Wm. & Mary. Capt. Mingiam.
(*d*) 30th. June 1684. Perygreen Coake. (Abra. Bayly.)

(*a*) A.832. Elizabeth Bird (?). 14. X.
(*b*) Georg Clark of Stepeny. Mariner.
(*c*) Carolina. 5.
(*d*) 30th. June 1684. (Abra. Bayly.)
This girl was taken out of Whitechappell Goal or Bridewell whether I had committed her for pilfering lace & sent by ye request of her father & Mother as Mr. Guy can testify.

(*a*) D.833. Edward Esmond, son of Edward Esmond from Broadworth (?) co. Wiltshire. About 24 years. A Taylor. Signs.
(*b*) John Bright of London. Merchant.
(*c*) Virginia. 4. To serve as a Taylor. Booth. Capt. Peter Pagan.
(*d*) Last day of June 1684. (No witness.) (Abra. Bayly.)

(*a*) A.834. William Wendright. 24. X.
(*b*) John Dodson of London. Merchant.

(c) Maryland. 4.
(d) 1st. July 1684. William Beale. (Abra. Bayly.)
    This man was brought out of prison at Whitechapple and his desch (? discharge) paid by his Transporter.

(a) A.835. Thomas Bummer. 25. Signs " Tho. Bumer ".
(b) John Dodsworth of London. Merchant.
(c) Maryland. 4.
(d) 1st. July 1684. William beale. (Abra. Bayly.)
    This man was taken out of Bridwell where he had layn.

(a) D.836. Robert Harrison. A Ploughman. Aged about 28. From Godmanchester, co. Huntingdon. Son of John Harrison. X.
(b) Francis Parties of London. Merchant.
(c) Mariland. 4. To serve as a Ploughman. Benedict Leonard. Capt. Francis Parties.
(d) 1st. July, 1684. John Shawe (?) (Abra. Bayly.)

(a) A.837. John Bullock. 25. Signs " John Bulluke".
(b) Isaack Lyon of London. Marriner.
(c) Virginia. 4.
(d) 2nd. July 1686. Henry Kentt. (Abra. Bayly.)

(a) A.838. John Stanton. 17. X.
(b) Richard Bayly of Mariland. Boatwright.
(c) Maryland. 7.
(d) 2nd. July 1684. Mark of William Sykes. (Abra. Bayly. W. Smyth.)

(a) A.839. Sarah Hilton. 16. X.
(b) Charles Parle of London. Marriner.
(c) Maryland. 4.
(d) 4th. July 1684. (Examined in the presence of her one Mother who is willing to her going, her father being dead, & is a witness hereto before me a Justice of peace for Middlesex. Abra. Bayly.)
    The mark of her own Mother Elizabeth Hill (*sic*).

(a) D.840. William B .... (?) son of William B .... (?) from Bullick co. Northampton. Aged about 28. A Gardner. X.
(b) Edward Burford of London. Merchant.
(c) Mariland. 4. To serve as a Gardner. Abraham & Francis. Capt. Edward Burford.
(d) 4th. July 1684. 2s. 6d. with him. John Ashby. (Abra. Bayly.)

(a) A.841. Lidea Pike. 22. X.
(b) Jacob Acres & Thomas Jordain of Limehows. Mariners.
(c) Maryland. 4.
(d) 6th. July 1684. Mark of Thomas Atkins. (Abra. Bayly.)

(*a*) D.842. John Curren. A Groome. Aged about 21. From Kelkenney in the Kingdom of Ireland. Son of William Curren. X.
(*b*) ffrancis Parties of London. Merchant.
(*c*) Mariland. 4. To serve as a Groome. Benedick Leanard. Capt. ffrancis Parties.
(*d*) 1st. July 1684. William Goodbourne. Richard Waring. (Abra. Bayly.)

(*a*) A.843. Samuell Champly. 25. Signs " Samuell Champley."
(*b*) Perrigrine Browne of London. Merchant.
(*c*) Maryland. 4.
(*d*) 7th. July 1684. (No Witness.) (Abra. Bayly.)

(a) A.844. Arabella Tempest. 22. X.
(*b*) Luis Evans of Maryland. Planter.
(*c*) Maryland. 5.
(*d*) 7th. July (1684). Wm. Evans. William beale. (Abra. Bayly.)

(*a*) A.845. Richard Norcolt. 14. X.
(*b*) Robert Hatton of East Smithfeild. Marriner.
(*c*) Maryland. 10.
(*d*) 7th. July 1684. (Witnesses) His one Mother & Brother, his father being dead, who is willing to his going. Mark of An Norcot. Mark of Henry Norcot. (Abra. Bayly.)

(*a*) D.846. David Oglevie. A Schollar. About 21. From Banff in the Kingdom of Scotland. Son of Allexander Oglevie. Signs " David Oglvie ".
(*b*) ffrancis Parties of London. Merchant.
(*c*) Mariland. 4. To serve as a Schollar. Benedict Leonard. Capt. ffrancis Parties.
(*d*) 7th. July 1684. John Richards. (Abra. Bayly.)

(*a*) D.847. Mary Goldsmith. Daughter of Henry Lester from Southwark, co. Surrey. 30. A widow. For housholdworke. X.
(*b*) Edward Talbott of London. Merchant.
(*c*) Mariland. 4. To serve on Howsholdworke. Adventure. Capt. Ralph Cooper.
(*d*) 9th. July 1684. The Mark of Henry Lester. The mark of Sarah Lester, being her one Mother. (Abra. Bayly.)

(*a*) D.848. Luke Williams. Aged about 28. From the Parish or place of Clandisent, in co. Carmarthen. A Groome. Son of John Jones. X.
(*b*) John Bright of London. Merchant.
(*c*) Maryland. 4. To serve as a Groome. Booth. Capt. Peter Pagan.
(*d*) 9th. July 1684. John Person. (Abra. Bayly.)

(*a*) D.849. Stephen Wright. A Husbandman. Aged about 22. From Prebey (?) co. Lincoln. Son of Stephen Wright. X.
(*b*) ffrancis Parties of London. Merchant.
(*c*) Mariland. 4. To serve as a Husbandman. Benedict Leonard. Capt. ffrancis Parties.
(*d*) 9th. July 1684. John Williams. (Abra. Bayly.)

(*a*) A.850. John Croffts. 32. X.
(*b*) Richard Moss of London. Merchant.
(*c*) Maryland. 4.
(*d*) 10th. July 1684. William Beale. (Abra. Bayly.)

(No. 851 is missing.)

(*a*) A.852. Joyce Harvey. 25. X.
(*b*) Luis Evans of Maryland. Planter.
(*c*) Maryland. 4.
(*d*) 11th. July 1684. William Beale. (Abra. Bayly.)

(*a*) A.853. John Robinson. 28. X.
(*b*) Jonas Cock of Wappen (i.e. Wapping). Carpenter.
(*c*) Maryland. 4.
(*d*) 11th. July 1684. William Beale. (Abra. Bayly.)

(*a*) D.854. John Baly, son of Launcelott Baly, from Todicke, co. Derby. Aged about 21. A Groome.
(*b*) John Bright of London. Merchant.
(*c*) Virginia. 4. To serve as a Groome. Booth. Capt. Peter Pagan.
(*d*) 11th. July 1684. John Williams. Richard Waring. (Abra. Bayly.)

(*a*) A.855. William Gurlin. 14. Signs.
(*b*) Daniel Clapham of Whitechappell. Marriner.
c) Virginia. 6.
(*d*) 14th. July 1684. (Abra. Bayly.)
    The Mark of Susanna Stokes his one mother who is willing to his going his father being dead.
    William Pinkard his Master to whom he was bound prentice & is willing to his going.
    The Mark of Thomas Stokes his father in law who consents to his going.

(*a*) A.856. John Stennet. 46. Signs " John Stennitt ".
(*b*) Michael Yoakly of London. Mariner.
(*c*) Maryland. 4.
(*d*) 14th. July 1684. Guy Wilson. (Abra. Bayly.)

(*a*) A.857. Thomas Darnel. 26. Signs " Thomas Darnell".
(*b*) Richard Molborn of Stepney. Mariner.

(c) Maryland. 4.
(d) 15th. July 1684. The Mark of Ann Marlborow. (Abra. Bayly.)

(a) D.858. Michael Drummer. Son of ffrancis Drummer from Brandborough, in the co. of High Holland. 21. A Labourer. X.
(b) ffrancis Parties of London. Merchant.
(c) Mariland. 4. To serve as a Labourer. Benedict Leonard. Capt. ffrancis Parties.
(d) 16th. July 1684. William goodbourn. Joseph P . . . . . . (?) (Abra. Bayly.)

(a) D.859. Benjamin Rose. Son of John Rose from Selby co. Yorke. 16. A ffriendless person. X.
(b) Edward Burford of London. Merchant.
(c) Mariland. 6. Abraham & Francis. Capt. Edward Burford.
(d) 16th. July 1684. Tho: Huttchens. George Hill. (Abra. Bayly. Ro: Hastings.)

(a) A.860. Mary Busby. 18. X.
(b) ffrancis Partis of London. Marriner.
(c) Maryland. 5.
(d) 17th. July 1684. The mark X of her one Mother Margret Busby, her father being dead as she saith upon oath. (Abra. Bayly. Ro: Hastings.)

(a) A.861. Frances Clark. 15. X.
(b) ffrancis Partis of London. Marriner.
(c) Maryland. 5.
(d) 17th. July 1684. The mark X of her one Mother Elizabeth Clark, her father being dead as appears uppon her oath. (Abra. Bayly. Ro: Hastings.)

(a) D.862. Richard Elletts son of Robert Elletts from Botherton co. Salop (?). 28. A Ploughman. X.
(b) Charles Parties of London. Merchant.
(c) Mariland. 4. To serve as a Ploughman. Potomock Merchant. Capt. Charles Parties.
(d) 18th. July 1684. John Williams. (Abra. Bayly.)

(a) A.863. Mary Langston. 14. X.
(b) John Jefcole (?) of London. Marriner.
(c) Virginia. 6.
(d) 18th. July 1684. Her one Mother is a witness hereto her father being dead X Easter her Mother. The mark X of Elizabeth Beasly. (Abra. Bayly. Ro: Hastings.)

(a) D.864. Jane Smith daughter of Wm. Smith from Rotha..our (?) co. York. About 24. A Spinster. X.
(b) Charles Parties of London. Merchant.

(c) Mariland. 4. Potomark Merchant. Capt. Charles Parties.
(d) 19th. July 1684. John Smith. (Abra. Bayly.)
(a) D.865. Richard Mullinex son of John Mullinex from Wiggon co. Lancaster. 13. A Husbandman. X.
(b) John Haselwood of London. Merchant.
(c) Mariland. 4. Golden Lyon. Capt. Longman.
(d) 19th. July 1684. Abraham Harris. (Abra. Bayly.)
(a) A.866. Ambros Wigelsworth. 24. Signs.
(b) Thomas Morley of Barbadoes. Planter.
(c) Barbadoes. 4.
(d) 21st. July 1684. William Beale. (Abra. Bayly.)
(a) A.867. Richard Peacock. 32. Signs.
(b) Richard Moss of London. Merchant.
(c) Maryland. 4.
(d) 23rd. July 1684. The mark X of Peter Howard. (Abra. Bayly.)
(a) D.868. Peter Snelling son of John Snelling from Pickadella co. Middx. 16. X.
(b) Edward Burford of London. Merchant.
(c) Mariland. 5. Abraham & ffrancis. Capt. Edward Burford.
(d) 23rd. July 1684. The mark X of John Snelling
the father. The mark X of Cornelia Snelling
the mother. John Person. (Abra. Bayly.)
His one father & mother as she maid oath wear present at my examination & consented.
(a) D.869. Richard Edgar son of Richard Edgar from . . . co. Middx. 27. A Ropemaker. X.
(b) Edward Burford of London. Merchant.
(c) Mariland. 4. To serve as a Ropemaker. Abraham & ffrancis. Capt. Edward Burford.
(d) 24th. July 1684. John Smith. (Abra. Bayly.)
(a) D.870. Seth Everill son of Seth Everill from the Parish or place of Shrusbury co. Salopp. 15. X.
(b) Edward Talbott of London. Merchant.
(c) Mariland. 8. Adventure. Capt. Ralph Cooper.
(d) 26th. July 1684. Tho. Hutchens. (Abra. Bayly. Ro: Hastings.)
(a) (Wording as A but slightly different form) 871. William Strowd son of Robert Strowd, who was present at his binding. 14. X.
(b) Michael Staples of Stepney. Marriner.
(c) Maryland. 7.
(d) 28th. July 1684. William Beale. Robert Strowde. (Abra. Bayly.)
(a) (As 871) 872. William Horton. 18. Son of William Horton, who was present at his binding & consents as likewise his one Mother. X.

(*b*) Thomas Newbold of London. Merchant.
(*c*) Maryland. 5.
(*d*) 28th. July 1684. The mark X of William Horton his father. (Abra. Bayly.)

(*a*) (As 871) 873. Deborah ffalconer daughter of Robert & Sarah ffalconer who were present at her binding. 19. X.
(*b*) Daniel Clapam Sen. (?) of London. Merchant.
(*c*) Maryland. 4.
(*d*) 28th. July 1684. Roert (*sic*) falkner. (Abra. Bayly.) The mark X of Sarah her Mother.

(*a*) D.874. Richard Swann. About 16. From Dublin, Ireland. Son of Richard Swann, Deceased. X.
(*b*) ffrancis Parties of London. Merchant.
(*c*) Mariland. 7. Benedict Leonard. Capt. ffrancis Parties.
(*d*) 30th. July 1684. Joseph Swan his one Brother who consents to his going, his father being dead & Mother in Ireland & willing. (Abra. Bayly.)

(*a*) A.875. William Townsend. About 18. X.
(*b*) James Galwith.
(*c*) Maryland. 4.
(*d*) 1st. August 1684. Symon Rawbone. George Harmer. (Tho: Hariot.) Sealed with an armorial seal. (Uncertain).

(*a*) A.876. Mary Gilbert. 20. X. With the Consent of her one Mother and father in law, present at her examination.
(*b*) William Johnson of London. Marriner.
(*c*) Maryland. 5.
(*d*) 1st. August 1684. The mark X of Elen Davis her one mother. William Beale. (Abra. Bayly.)

(*a*) A.877. John Curtis. 30. X.
(*b*) Bartholomew Watts of London. Marriner.
(*c*) Maryland. 4. His dubble apparell is to be of Broadcloth or Kersey.
(*d*) 4th. August 1684. Anthony Pryar (?) (Abra. Bayly.)

(*a*) A.878. Charles Siviter. 12. X.
(*b*) Abraham Clark of Maryland. Planter.
(*c*) Maryland. 9.
(*d*) 5th. August 1684. The mark X of his one father Richard Siviter. The mark X of Elizabeth Siviter his one Mother Who boath weer present at his examination & wear willing to his going. William Beale. (Abra. Bayly.)

(*a*) A.879. Richard Chapman. 30. X.
(*b*) Richard Batt of London. Merchant.
(*c*) Maryland. 4.
(*d*) 5th. August 1684. William Beale. (Abra. Bayly.)

(a) (Special form printed in script type) 880. Mary Harris. About 21. X.
(b) Thomas Tench.
(c) Maryland. 5.
(d) 6th. August 1684. Samuel Merryhurst. Thomas Boys. (Thos. Hariot.)

(a) (As 880) 881. Edward Taylor of London. About 17. Signs.
(b) Thomas Tench.
(c) Maryland. 6.
(d) 6th. August 1684. Samuel Merryhurst. Thomas Boys. (Tho: Hariot.)

(a) A.882. Abraham Ogden son of Samuel Ogden who is present & consents to his binding. Signs.
(b) Michael Yokely of London. Marriner.
(c) Maryland. 8.
(d) 9th. August 1684. Richd. Moss and his one father Samuel Ogden. (Abra. Bayly.)

(a) A.883. John Greenwood. 21. X.
(b) Richard Moss of London. Merchant.
(c) Maryland. 4.
(d) 11th. August 1684. Richd. Parkines. (Abra. Bayly.)
This John Greenwood is a seaman that hath used the trade of going to Virginia.

(a) A.884. Jacob Barrownouch (?) a polander. 18. X.
(b) William King of London. Merchant.
(c) Maryland. 4.
(d) 11th. August 1684. Richd. Parkines. (Abra. Bayly.)

(a) A.885. Abigall Manning. 30. Signs " Abigal Maning ".
(b) Thomas Bennett of London. Shipwright.
(c) Virginia. 4.
(d) 12th. August 1684. William Beale. (Abra. Bayly.)

(a) A.886. Susan Arden. 15, whos one father is present & witness hereto. X.
(b) Edmond Sandeford, planter.
(c) Barbadoes. 5.
(d) 13th. August 1684. John Arding her one father. (Abra. Bayly.)

(a) D.887. Wm. Jackson. A Husbandman. 30. Son of Mathew Jackson, dead. From Hincksorne (?) co. Cambridge. X.
(b) Thomas Arnall of London. Merchant.
(c) Virginia. 4. To serve as a Husbandman. Jefferies. Capt. Thomas Arnall.
(d) 13th. August 1684. Richard Waring. (Abra. Bayly.)

(a) D.888. Thomas Luke. A Husbandman. 30. Son of William Luke Deceased from Beasly co. Gloscester. X.

(b) Thomas Arnall of London. Merchant.
(c) Virginia. 5. To serve as a Husbandman. Jefferies. Capt. Thomas Arnoll.
(d) 13th. August 1684. Joseph Pycraft. (Abra. Bayly.)

(a) A.889. Oliver Palmer. 15. X.
(b) William ffrisby of Maryland. Merchant.
(c) Maryland. 7.
(d) 14th. August 1684. Two of his one uncles his father & Mother being dead & he no apprentice as they say upon oath. Hen: Nicholls. Thomas Palmer. (Abra. Bayly.)

(a) A.890. ffrances Bauldwin. 16. Signs " Frances Baldwin ".
(b) Bartholomew Oates of London. Mariner.
(c) Maryland. 5.
(d) 14th. August 1684. An Billion & John Ewbanck who upon oath saith her father is dead & her mother willing to her going. John Ewbancke. William Beale. (Abra. Bayly.)

(a) A.891. Mathew Swanson. 25. Signs " Matthew Swansone ".
(b) Thomas Grubb of Rotherith. Marriner.
(c) Virginia. 4.
(d) 14th. August 1684. William Beale. (Abra. Bayly.)
    Debett 1s.

(a) D.892. Wm. Alligin. A labourer. 30. Son of Robert Alligin dead. From Cophill, co. Essex. X.
(b) Thomas Arnall of London. Merchant.
(c) Virginia. 4. Jefferies. Capt. Thomas Arnall.
(d) 14th. August 1684. Nath: Randell. John Richards. (Abra. Bayly.) Rich. Dealle.

(a) A.893. Jacob ffrancis a dutchman. 34. X.
(b) William Haviland of London. Merchant.
(c) Virginia. 4.
(d) 15th. August 1684. Rob. Shanke. (Abra. Bayly.)

(a) D.894. Phillip Dycer. A Taylor. 29. Son of Phillipp Dycer from Flushing in Zealand. Signs.
(b) John Moore of London. Merchant.
(c) Virginia. 4. To serve as a Taylor. Assistance. Capt. James Strong.
(d) 15th. August 1684. Richard Waring. (Abra. Bayly.)

(a) A.895. William Edmons. Signs.
(b) Peter Greene of London.
(c) Virginia. 5.
(d) 16th. August 1684. Max: Robinson. John Pettit. (Tho: Hariot.)

(a) A.896. William Hanly. 28. X.
(b) Richard Batt of London. Merchant.
(c) Virginia. 4.
(d) 18th. August 1684. Nath: Randell. (Abra. Bayly.)

(a) D.897. George King, by the Mother's consent. 18. From St. Buttolph without Allgate, co. Middx. X.
(b) John Bright of London. Merchant.
(c) Virginia. 5. Assistance. Capt. James Strong.
(d) 18th. August 1684. Grace King the Mother, X her mark. (Abra. Bayly. Ro: Hastings.)

(a) D.898. Thomas Brigdon. 16. Son of Wm. Brigdon, deceased, from Hell...(?) in co. Sussex. X.
(b) Thomas Arnall of London. Merchant.
(c) Virginia. 7. Jefferies. Capt. Thomas Arnall.
(d) 19th. August 1684. (No witnesses.) (Abra. Bayly. Ro: Hastings.) Debett Mr. Richerson.

(a) A.899. Ffrances Darrant. 18. Her mark X.
(b) John Twilt of London. Marriner.
(c) Maryland. 4.
(d) 18th. August 1684. Richd. Parkines. (Abra. Bayly. Ro: Hastings.)

(a) A.900. James Bower. 18. X.
(b) Abraham Wild of London. Merchant.
(c) Maryland. 6.
(d) 18th. August 1684. William Beale. (Abra. Bayly. Ro: Hastings.)

(a) A.901. Thomas Cary. 15. From the hows of Correction. (? Signs.)
(b) Christopher Daniell of London. Marriner.
(c) Maryland. 9.
(d) 19th. August 1684. William Beale. (Abra. Bayly. Ro: Hastings.)

(a) A.902. John Collins. 30. Signs.
(b) Thomas Jennings of Popler. Marriner.
(c) Maryland. 4.
(d) 19th. August 1684. William Beale. (Abra. Bayly.)

(a) A.903. Mary Bennett. 18. X.
(b) Abraham Wild of London. Merchant.
(c) Maryland. 4.
(d) 19th. August 1684. William Beale. (Abra. Bayly. Ro: Hastings.)

(a) D.904. Mary Evans. Spinster. 19. Dau. of William Evans, deceased, from Broad, co. Stafford. X.

(b) Thomas Arnall of London. Merchant.
(c) Virginia. 4. Jefferies. Capt. Thomas Arnall.
(d) 19th. August 1684. George Dance. (Abra. Bayly. Ro: Hastings.)

(a) D.905. Richard Hillard. A Groome. 19. Son of Peter Hillard, living, from Arpithe, co. Dorsetshire. X.
(b) John Bright of London. Merchant.
(c) Virginia. 5. To serve as a Groome. Assistance. Capt. James Strong.
(d) 20th. August 1684. Nicholas Woolfe. (Abra. Bayly. Ro: Hastings.)

(a) D.906. Richard Rose. A Husbandman. 31. Son of Richard Rose from Mansester, co. Warwickshire. Signs.
(b) John Bright of London. Merchant.
(c) Virginia. 4. To serve as a Husbandman. Assistance. Capt. James Strong.
(d) 20th August 1684. Tho. W... (?).... (?) Lorries (?). (Abra. Bayly.)

(a) D.907. John Billing. 18. Son of John Billing Decd. from Finnwell (?), co. Rutland. X.
(b) John Bright of London. Merchant.
(c) Mariland. 6. Assistance. Capt. James Strong.
(d) 21st. August 1684. Symon Robinson. John Williams. (Abral Bayly. Ro: Hastings.)

(a) D.908. Thomas Correy. A Tanner. 23. Son of Archabal. Correy from the City and County of Chester. Signs.
(b) John Bright of London. Merchant.
(c) Mariland. 4. Assistance. Capt. James Strong.
(d) 21st. August 1684. Redmond Correy. John Richards. (Abra. Bayly.)

(a) A.909. Robert Johnson. 30. X.
(b) Richard Batt of London. Merchant.
(c) Virginia. 4.
(d) 21st. August 1684. John Richards. (Abra. Bayly.)

(a) D.910. Thomas Lolley. 21. Son of John Lolling [sic.]. Signs "Thomas Lolley".
(b) John Bright of London. Merchant.
(c) Mariland. 4. Assistance. Capt. James Strong.
(d) 21st. August 1684. Gilbert Brown. (Abra. Bayly.)

(a) D.911. ffrancis Barker. Labourer. 21. Son of R .. en (?) Barker, from London.
(b) Thomas Arnall of London. Merchant.

(c) Virginia. 5. Jefferies. Capt. Thomas Arnall.
(d) 21st August 1684. (No witnesses.) (Abra. Bayly.)

(a) D.912. John Brooks. A Blacksmith. 24. Son of John Brooks decd., from Woolingstock (?), co. Worcester. X.
(b) Thomas Arnall of London. Merchant.
(c) Virginia. 5. To serve as a Blacksmith. Jefferies. Capt. Thomas Arnall.
(d) 21st. August 1684. Edmd. Pattman. (Abra. Bayly.)

(a) A.913. Peter Geay. About 20 years. Signs.
(b) Richard Bray.
(c) Maryland. 4. "Working in the ground excepted".
(d) 22nd. August 1684. Samuel Barbat. Andrew Bunion. (Tho: Hariot.)

(a) A.914. Mary Atwell. 22. Signs "Mary atewill".
(b) John Twilt of London. Merchant.
(c) Maryland. 4.
(d) 22nd. August 1684. William Beale. (Abra. Bayly.)

(a) D.915. Wm. Roger. Ploughman. 21. Son of Walter Roger. Signs.
(b) Thomas Arnall of London. Merchant.
(c) Virginia. 5. To serve as a Ploughman. Jefferies. Capt. Thomas Arnall.
(d) 22nd. August 1684. The Mark X of Symon Robinson. John Williams. (Abra. Bayly.)

(a) D.916. Henry Brisco. 21. Son of Henry Brisco, Living. From Tamworth in the county of Warwicks. Signs "Henery Brisco."
(b) Thomas Arnall of London. Merchant.
(c) Virginia. 6. Jefferies. Capt. Thomas Arnall.
(d) 22nd. August 1684. Jno. Dix. (Abra. Bayly.)

(a) D.917. Elizabeth Lawton, spinster. 21. Daughter of Wm. Lawton, Living. From the County and City of Lincoln. X.
(b) Thomas Arnall of London. Merchant.
(c) Virginia. 5. Jefferies. Capt. Thomas Arnall.
(d) 22nd. August 1684. John Cooke. (Abra. Bayly.)

(a) D.918. Alice Stevens, spinster. 18. Daughter of John Stevens from London. X.
(b) John Bright of London. Merchant.
(c) Virginia. 5. Assistance. Capt. James Strong.
(d) 22nd. August 1684. Tho: Hutchens. (Abra. Bayly. Ro: Hastings.)

(a) D.919. John Morrell. Gardner. 22. Son of Wm. Morrell from Stock parish in the County of Stafford. Signs " John Morrall".
(b) Thomas Arnall of London. Merchant.
(c) Virginia. 4. To serve as a Gardner. Jefferies. Capt. Thomas Arnall.
(d) 22nd. August 1684. Samuell Barker. Edwd. Loveis (?). (Abra. Bayly.) This same person was bound before and his Indenture delivered in and afterwards three (?) & now bound againe. Debett Mr. Haveland.

(a) A.920. Edward Nelson. 23. Signs.
(b) John Twilt of London. Merchant.
(c) Maryland. 4.
(d) 23rd. August 1684. The mark X of Edward Sapsford. (Abra. Bayly.)

(a) D.921. David Williams. A Husbandman. 31. Son of Wm. Williams from Mold in the county of Flintshire. Signs.
(b) John Bright of London. Merchant.
(c) Mariland. 4. To serve as a Husbandman. Assistance. Capt. James Stong.
(d) 23rd. August 1684. Elliz. Thomas. (Abra. Bayly.)

(a) A.922. John Ball. 23. X.
(b) Thomas Berrisford of London. Merchant.
(c) Virginia. 4.
(d) 23rd. August 1684. William Beale. (Abra. Bayly.)

(a) A.923. Mary Hastings. 23 or thereabouts. X.
(b) Richard Bray.
(c) Maryland. 4.
(d) 25th. August 1684. The mark X of Elizabeth Evans. John Pettit. (Tho: Hariot.)

(a) A.924. Elizabeth Mercer. 29. X.
(b) Samuell Williams of London. Shipwright.
(c) Virginia. 4.
(d) 25th. August 1684. William Beale. (Abra. Bayly.) Debett a shilling.

(a) A.925. Charles Winter. 22. X.
(b) Moses ffulborne of London. Marriner.
(c) Maryland. 4.
(d) 25th August 1684. William Beale. (Abra. Bayly.)

(a) A.926. Jane Trunkett. 30. X.
(b) Thomas Berisford of London. Marriner.
(c) Virginia. 4.
(d) 25th. August 1684. John ffreeman. (Abra. Bayly.)

(*a*) A.927. John Hadely (also spelt Hadley). X.
(*b*) Thomas Berrisford of London. Marriner.
(*c*) Virginia. 4.
(*d*) 25th. August 1684. John ffreeman. (Abra. Bayly.)

(*a*) D.928. James Markley. 22. Son of James Markley from Ayre in the Kingdom of France. X.
(*b*) John Bright of London. Merchant.
(*c*) Mariland. 5. Assistance. Capt. James Strong.
(*d*) 25th. August 1684. John Dix. (Abra. Bayly.)

(*a*) D.929. John Reeve. A Feltmaker. 32. Son of Edward Reeve from Watford in the county of Northampton. Signs.
(*b*) John Bright of London. Merchant.
(*c*) Mariland. 4. To serve as a Feltmaker. Assistance. Capt. James Strong.
(*d*) 25th. August 1684. Tho. Hatcherd. (Abra. Bayly.) 5s. with him.

(*a*) D.930. James Wood a Tayler. 20. Son of Wm. Wood from Weschester. Signs.
(*b*) Thomas Arnall of London. Merchant.
(*c*) Virginia. 4. To serve as a Tailor. Jefferies. Capt. Thomas Arnall.
(*d*) 25th. August 1684. (No witnesses.) (Abra. Bayly. Ro: Hastings.) 10s. with him.

(*a*) D.931. Peter Davison. 22. Son of John Davison from Dundee in the Kingdom of Scotland. X.
(*b*) John Bright of London. Merchant.
(*c*) Mariland. 5. Assistance. Capt. James Strong.
(*d*) 25th. August 1684. John Dix. (Abra. Bayly.)

(*a*) A.932. ffrances Atkinson. 22 or thereabouts. X.
(*b*) Richard Bray.
(*c*) Mary Land. 4.
(*d*) 26th. August 1684. Jno. Heyricke. The mark X of Gulielmi Brees. (Tho: Hariot.)

(*a*) A.933. ffrances Hildridg. 28. X.
(*b*) Thomas Berrisford of London. Marriner.
(*c*) Virginia. 4.
(*d*) 26th. August 1684. William Beale. Charles Broughton. (Abra. Bayly.)

(*a*) D.934. Thomas Kynner. A Sawyer. 40. Son of Edward Kynner, from Worksey (?), co. Wilts. X.
(*b*) John Bright of London. Merchant.
(*c*) Mariland. 4. To serve as a Sawyer. Assistance. Capt. James Strong.

(*d*) 26th. August 1684. William goodbourne. (Abra. Bayly.) 5s. with him.

(*a*) D.935. Nicholas Cock. About 21. From Exeter, co. Devon. Son of John Cock. X.
(*b*) John Bright of London. Merchant.
(*c*) Mariland. 4. Assistance. Capt. James Strong.
(*d*) 26th. August 1684. The mark X of John Richards. (Abra. Bayly.) Debett.

(*a*) A.936. Nicholas Smyth. 19. Signs " Nicolas Smith ".
(*b*) Maximilian Robinson of London. Merchant.
(*c*) Virginia. 6.
(*d*) 26th. August 1684. Thomas Shepheard. (Abra. Bayly. Ro: Hastings.)

(*a*) D.937. Benjamin Kett. A Barber. 19. From Norwich, co. Norfolk. Son of Henry Kett. Signs.
(*b*) John Bright of London. Merchant.
(*c*) Mariland. 5. To serve as a Barber. Assistance. Capt. James Strong.
(*d*) 26th. August 1684. Joseph Pycraft. (Abra. Bayly. Ro: Hastings.)

(*a*) D.938. John Crackwell. 21. From Burrowgreene, co. Cambridge. Son of Richard Crockwell. X.
(*b*) John Bright of London. Merchant.
(*c*) Mariland. 4. Assistance. Capt. James Strong.
(*d*) 26th. August 1684. John Richards. (Abra. Bayly.)

(*a*) A.939. Cathrine Harding. 21. X.
(*b*) William Ballard of London. Shipwright.
(*c*) Virginia. 4.
(*d*) 26th. August 1684. The mark X of Margrett Higgins. (Abra. Bayly.)

(*a*) D.940. Joseph Honywell. Accomptant. 30. Son of Wm. Honneywell from St. Austin, co. Cornwall. Signs " Joseph Hunnywill ".
(*b*) John Bright of London. Merchant.
(*c*) Mariland. 4. To serve as an Accomptant. Assistance. Capt. James Strong.
(*d*) 26th. August 1684. William Lyes. (Abra. Bayly.)

(*a*) D.941. Wm. Lyle. Barber Chirurgion. 22. From Whickham in the County of Durham. Son of Thomas Lyle. Signs.
(*b*) John Carter of London. Merchant.
(*c*) Virginia. 4. To serve as a Barber Chirurgeon. Jefferies. Capt. Thomas Arnall.
(*d*) 26th. August 1684. William Pe . . kin (?). Edmd. Loweing (?). (Abra. Bayly.)

(*a*) D.942. Edward Clayton. About 32. From Berkshire. X.
(*b*) John Carter of London. Merchant.
(*c*) Virginia. 4. To serve as a Husbandman. Jefferies. Capt. Thomas Arnall.
(*d*) 26th. August 1684. James Kingsland. (Abra. Bayly.)

(*a*) A.943. Jacob Morris. 14. Born in France. Signs " Jacob Mories ".
(*b*) Nicholas Pamle of Maryland, gent.
(*c*) Mariland. 7.
(*d*) 27th. August 1684. William Beale. (Abra. Bayly.)

(*a*) D.944. Ellioner Barnes. Spinster. 21. From the county of Middx. Daughter of James Barnes. X.
(*b*) Thomas Hasteed of London. Merchant.
(*c*) Mariland. 4. Recoverie. Capt. Thomas Hasteed.
(*d*) 27th. August 1684. Edwd. Loweing (?). (Abra. Bayly.)

(*a*) D.945. Thomas Grindy. A Farmer. 23. Son of Phillipp Grindy from Cardiff in the county of Glomargan. X.
(*b*) John Carter of London. Merchant.
(*c*) Virginia. 4. To serve as a Farmer. Jefferies. Capt. Thomas Arnall.
(*d*) 27th. August 1684. James Williams. (Abra. Bayly.)

(*a*) D.946. John ffloyd. 18. Son of John ffloyd from Nighton, co. Hereford. (? Knighton, co. Radnor.) X.
(*b*) John Bright of London. Merchant.
(*c*) Mariland. 4. Assistance. Capt. James Strong.
(*d*) 27th. August 1684. William Lyes (?). (Abra. Bayly. Ro: Hastings.)

(*a*) D.947. Edmund Hudson. 19. Son of John Hudson from Northarlarton, co. Yorke. (Northallerton.) Signs.
(*b*) John Carter of London. Merchant.
(*c*) Virginia. 4. Jefferies. Capt. Thomas Arnall.
(*d*) 27th. August 1684. Andrew Whining. (Abra. Bayly. Ro: Hastings.) 5£ with him.

(*a*) D.948. Richard Swaisland. A Groome. 22. Son of Henry Swaisland from Seell (Seal), co. Kent. X. (Name also spelt Swasland and Swailsland.)
(*b*) Thomas Hasteed of London. Merchant.
(*c*) Mariland. 4. To serve as a Groome. Recoverie. Capt. Thomas Hasteed.
(*d*) 27th. August 1684. Richard Waring. (Abra. Bayly.)

(*a*) A.949. James Hiland. 29. Signs " James Hyland ".
(*b*) Nicholas Painter of Maryland, gent.
(*c*) Maryland. 4.
(*d*) 27th. August 1684. William Beale. (Abra. Bayly.)

(*a*) A.950. John German. 21. X.
(*b*) Nicholas Painter of Maryland, gent.
(*c*) Maryland. 4.
(*d*) 27th. August 1684. William Beale. (Abra. Bayly.)

(*a*) A.951. Margaret prou. 24 Or thereabouts. X.
(*b*) Richard Bray.
(*c*) Virginia. 4. " Working in the Ground excepted ".
(*d*) 28th. August 1684. Samuel Barbat. Jacob Mailhet. (Tho: Hariot.) (Sealed in red wax. A tree between the letters C.P.).

(*a*) A.952. Cyprian Prou. 21, or thereabouts. Signs " Ciprien Prou ".
(*b*) Richard Bray.
(*c*) Virginia. 4. " Working in the ground excepted."
(*d*) 28th. August 1684. Samuel Barbat. Jacob Mailhet. (Tho: Hariot.) (Same seal as No. 951.)

(*a*) D.953. John Tomkin. A Groom. 28. Son of John Tomkin from Denton in the county of Bedford. Signs.
(*b*) Thomas Hasteed of London. Merchant.
(*c*) Mariland. 4. To serve as a Groom. Recoverie. Capt. Thomas Hasteed.
(*d*) 28th. August 1684. X. Mark of Thomas Winn. John Richards. (Abra. Bayly.) 10£ with him.

(*a*) A.954 John Hawe. 25. Signs " John Hall."
(*b*) John Twilt of London. Marriner.
(*c*) Maryland. 4.
(*d*) 28th. August 1684. William Beale. (Abra. Bayly.)

(*a*) A.955. Thomas Mathews. 18. X.
(*b*) John More of London. Merchant.
(*c*) Virginia. 6.
(*d*) 28th. August 1684. William Beale. (Abra. Bayly. Ro: Hastings.)

(*a*) A.956. John Robinson. 21. Signs " John Robson ".
(*b*) William Webb of Ratcliff. Shipwright.
(*c*) Virginia. 4.
(*d*) 28th. August 1684. John Tanner. (Abra. Bayly.)

(*a*) D.957. George Laurence (?). 31. Son of William Laurence (?). X.
(*b*) Thomas Hasteed of London. Merchant.
(*c*) Mariland. 4. Recoverie. Capt. Thomas Hasteed.
(*d*) 28th. August 1684. Edmund Pattmea (?). (Abra. Bayly.) 10£ with him.

(*a*) A.958. Walter English. 13. whose father is witness hereto. Signs.
(*b*) Samuel Berry, of Bow. Surgeon (?).

(c) Virginia. 7.
(d) 29th. August 1684. Walter English. (Abra. Bayly.)
(a) D.959. Moses Rest. A Husbandman. 26. Son of ffinch (?). Rest from . . . llington (?) in the county of Kent. X.
(b) John Carter of London. Merchant.
(c) Virginia. 5. Jefferies. Capt. Thomas Arnall.
(d) 29th. August 1684. Abraham Harris. (Abra. Bayly.)

(a) A.960. Sarah Parker. 24. X.
(b) Richard Jackson of Barbadoes. Merchant.
(c) Barbadoes. 3.
(d) 29th. August 1684. William Beale. (Abra. Bayly.)

(a) A.961. John Stokely. 16. X.
(b) Richard Bayly of Maryland. Planter.
(c) Maryland. 8.
(d) 29th. August 1684. Joseph Pycraft. (Abra. Bayly. Ro: Hastings.)

(a) D.962. Mary Stanton. Spinster. 17. Daughter of Phillipp Stanton from London. X.
(b) Thomas Hasteed of London. Merchant.
(c) Mariland. 4. Recoverie. Capt. Thomas Hasteed.
(d) 29th. August 1684. Richard Waring. (Abra. Bayly. Ro: Hastings.)

(a) A.963. Bozoun Goodrick. 26. Signs.
(b) Richard Jackson of Barbadoes. Merchant.
(c) Barbadoes. 3.
(d) 29th. August 1684. William Beale. (Abra. Bayly.)

(a) A.964. Thomas Williams. 13. Whose father in law is witness hereto. X.
(b) John Worthington of Maryland. Merchant.
(c) Maryland. 9.
(d) 30th. August 1684. His father in law his one father & mother being dead as appears uppon oath. X William Marry (?) his father in laws mark. (Abra. Bayly.)

(a) D.965. Thomas Dunkley of the parish of Newbale co. Lestesheire. 17. Signs.
(b) John Carter of London. Merchant.
(c) Virginia. 5. To serve as a Servant. Jefferies. Capt. Thomas Strong.
(d) 30th. August 1684. Nath: Randell. (Abra. Bayly. Ro: Hastings.)

(a) D.966. John Pewtow (?). 17. Son of John Pewtow (?) from Harrison co. Kent. X.
(b) Thomas Hasteed of London. Merchant.

(c) Mariland. 7. Recoverie. Capt. Thomas Hasteed.
(d) 30th. August 1684. William Peterkin. (Abra. Bayly. Ro: Hastings.)
(a) D.967. John Armstrong of the City of York. 15. X.
(b) John Carter of London. Merchant.
(c) Virginia. 6. To serve as a Servant. Jefferies. Capt. Thomas Strong.
(d) 30th. August 1684. Nath: Randell. (Abra. Bayly. Ro: Hastings.)
(a) D.968. Robert Steevens (?). 18. Son of John Steavens (?) from Banbury (?) co. Derby (?). X.
(b) John Bright of London. Merchant.
(c) Meriland. 7. Assistance. Capt. James Strong.
(d) 30th. August 1684. (No witness.) (Abra. Bayly. Ro: Hastings.)
(a) D.969. Nathanell Palmer. A Groome. 21. Son of Elizahias Palmer from Pippall Abby in co. Northampton. X.
(b) John Carter of London. Merchant.
(c) Virginia. 5. To serve as a Groome. Jefferies. Capt. Thomas Arnall.
(d) 30th. August 1684. William Peterkin. (Abra. Bayly.)
(a) A.970. ffrancis Coffin. 27. Signs (?).
(b) William Webb of Ratclif. Shipwright.
(c) Virginia. 4.
(d) last of August 1684. Richd. Parkines. (Abra. Bayly.)
(a) A.971. An Bancks. 22. X.
(b) Richard Bayly of Maryland. Planter.
(c) Maryland. 5.
(d) 1st September 1684. Christopher .... (?). (Abra. Bayly.)
(a) D.972. Joseph Banton. 17. Son of Charles Banton from Leeds co. York. Signs.
(b) John Carter of London. Merchant.
(c) Virginia. 7. Jefferies. Capt. Thomas Arnall.
(d) 1st. September 1684. John Williams. (Abra. Bayly. Ro: Hastings.)
(a) D.973. Anne Diptale. Singlewoman. 21. Daughter of John Diptale of the City of Bristol, Looking glass maker. X.
(b) Thomas Hastings of London. Merchant.
(c) Merryland in Virginia. 5. To serve as a Servant. Recoverie. Capt. Thomas Hastings.
(d) 1st. September 1684. John Richards. Tho. Cornelius. (Abra. Bayly. Ro: Hastings.)
(a) D.974. Edward Danby (?). A Groome. About 21. From Milton (?) co. Lancashire. Son of John Danby (?). X.
(b) John Carter of London. Merchant.

(*c*) Mariland. 5. To serve as a Groome. Jefferies. Capt. Thomas Arnall.
(*d*) 1st. September 1684. (No witness.) (Abra. Bayly.)

(*a*) Script Form, as No. 880. 975. Mary Richerson. 18. X.
(*b*) Richard Batt of London. Merchant.
(*c*) Maryland. 4.
(*d*) 1st. September 1684. John Richards. (Abra. Bayly. Ro: Hastings.)

(*a*) A.976. Elizabeth Grey. 21. X.
(*b*) John Brown of London. Mariner.
(*c*) Virginia. 4.
(*d*) 1st. September 1684. William Beale. (Abra. Bayly.)

(*a*) D.977. Sarah Lefeadero. Singlewoman. 16. Daughter of Charles Lefeadro of Layden in Holland. Dyer.
(*b*) Thomas Hastings of London. Merchant.
(*c*) Merryland. 7. To serve as a Servant. Recoverie. Capt. Thomas Hastings.
(*d*) 1st. September 1684. Nath: Randell. Tho. Cornelius. (Abra. Bayly. Ro: Hastings.)

(*a*) D.978. Wm. Bings. A Taylor. About 24. From Redford co. Notts. Son of Richard Bings. Signes " William Binges."
(*b*) John Moore of London. Merchant.
(*c*) Merriland. 4. To serve as a Taylor. Recoverie. Capt. Thomas Hasteed.
(*d*) 1st. September 1684. John Spring. (Abra. Bayly. Ro: Hastings.)

(*a*) D.979. John Baker. A Husbandman. About 21. From Waltonstone co. Essex. Son of Bartholomew Baker.
(*b*) John Moore of London. Merchant.
(*c*) Virginia. 4. Jefferies. Capt. Thomas Arnall.
(*d*) 2nd. September 1684. John Richards. Edwd. Lowery (?). (Abra. Bayly.)

(*a*) D.980. Wm. Carpenter. A Butcher. About 27. From Shipton upon Craven co. York. Son of Patrick Carpenter. X.
(*b*) John Moore of London. Merchant.
(*c*) Mariland. 4. To serve as a Butcher. Jefferies. Capt. Thomas Arnall.
(*d*) 2nd. September 1684. John Richards. Edwd. Lowery (?). (Abra. Bayly.)

(*a*) D.981. Hugh Jones of Flintshire. 21. The son of John Jones of the same Shire. X.
(*b*) Thomas Hastings of London. Merchant.

(c) Maryland. 4. To serve as a Servant. Recoverie. Capt. Thomas Hastings.
(d) 2nd. September 1684. William goodbourne. (Abra. Bayly.)

(a) D.982. Richard Holmes. A Cordwayner. 25. Son of Richard Holmes from Beudly co. Worcester. Signs.
(b) John Moore of London. Merchant.
(c) Mariland. 4. To serve as a Cordwayner. Hound. Capt. Hind.
(d) 2nd. September 1684. John Earle. (Abra. Bayly.)

(a) D.983. Robert Whitby. A Groome. About 24. From Helsby co. Chester. Son of Randall Whitby. X.
(b) John Carter of London. Merchant.
(c) Mariland. 4. To serve as a Groome. Jefferies. Capt. Thomas Arnall.
(d) 2nd. September 1684. William Peterkin. (Abra. Bayly.)

(a) A.984. An Hutton. 21. X.
(b) John Twilt of London. Merchant.
(c) Maryland. 4.
(d) 2nd. September 1684. William Beale. (Abra. Bayly.)

(a) A.985. Susan Hutton. 21. X.
(b) John Twilt of London. Marriner.
(c) Maryland. 4.
(d) 2nd. September 1684. William Beale. (Abra. Bayly.)

(a) A.986. John Naylor. 22. X.
(b) Nicholas Painter of London. Merchant.
(c) Maryland. 4.
(d) 2nd. September 1684. William Beale. (Abra. Bayly.)

(a) D.987. Thomas ffowler. 17. Son of Wm. ffowler from Milton Mowbray co. Lester. Friendless. Relies upon Church. . . . (?).
(b) John Moore of London. Merchant.
(c) Mariland or Virginia. 7. Recoverie. Capt. Thomas Hasteed.
(d) 2nd. September 1684. (No witness.) (Abra. Bayly. Ro: Hastings.)

(a) D.988. John Skinner. 21. From Weanenfield (?) co. Sussex. Son of Wm. Skinner. X.
(b) John Dix of London. Merchant.
(c) Mariland. 4. Hound. Capt. Hinde.
(d) 3rd. September 1684. Richard Smith. Edward Lowery (?) (Abra. Bayly.)

(a) D.989. Elizabeth Webb. Spinster. About 25. From Elston co. Gloucester. Daughter of Richard Webb. X.
(b) John Bowman of London. Merchant.

(c) Mariland. 4. Mary of London. Capt. John Harris.
(d) 3rd. September 1684. Edwd. Lowery (?). (Abra. Bayly.)

(a) D.990. Walter Wright. A Groome. About 22. From Whistone co. Northampton. Son of Wm. Wright. Signs.
(b) John Carter of London. Merchant.
(c) Virginia. 4. To serve as a Groome. Jefferies. Capt. Thomas Arnall.
(d) 3rd. September 1684. Joseph Pycraft. Edward Lowery (?). (Abra. Bayly.)

(a) A.991. Davie Williams. 18. X.
(b) Thomas Gadsden of London. Merchant.
(c) In Barbadoes. 4.
(d) 4th. September 1684. William Beale. (Abra. Bayly.)

(a) A.992. John Hall. 22. Signs.
(b) John Tannor, of Lime hows. Marriner.
(c) Virginia. 4.
(d) 4th. September 1684. James Pliner (?). (Abra. Bayly.)

(a) D.993. Arther Hancock. A Husbandman. About 28. From the City of Bristall. Son of Roger Hancock. Signs.
(b) John Bowman of London. Merchant.
(c) Mariland. 4. To serve as a Husbandman. Mary of London. Capt. John Harris.
(d) 4th. September 1684. Edwd. Lowery (?). (Abra. Bayly.)

(a) A.994. Charles Church. 38. Signs.
(b) Richard Jackson of Barbadoes. Merchant.
(c) In Barbadoes. 3.
(d) 4th. September 1684. William Beale. (Abra. Bayly.)

(a) A.995. Thomas Hern. 21. Signs " Thomas Hearne."
(b) Edward Brooks of London. Merchant.
(c) Jameca. 4.
(d) 4th. September 1684. Theop: Haydocke. (Abra. Bayly.)

(a) A.996. Margrett Ash. 21. X.
(b) Edward Brook of London. Merchant.
(c) In Jamaca. 4.
(d) 4th. September 1684. William Beale. (Abra. Bayly.)

(a) A.997. Mary Pelham. 21. X.
(b) Edward Brook of London. Merchant.
(c) In Jamaca. 4.
(d) 4th. September 1684. William Beale. (Abra. Bayly.)

(a) D.998. Wm. ffenwick. About 21. From Lincoln in the county of the same. Son of Robert ffenwick. Signs.
(b) Philles Hinde of London. Merchant.

(c) Mariland. 4. Hound. Capt. Philles Hinde.
(d) 4th. September 1684. Edwd. Lowery (?). (Abra. Bayly.)

(a) A.999. ffrederick Harris. 22. Signs.
(b) John Day of London. Merchant.
(c) Maryland. 4.
(d) 4th. September 1684. X mark of Peter Howard (?). (Abra. Bayly.)

(a) D.1000. John Darling. Cordwayner. 21. Son of John Darling in the Kingdom of Scotland. X.
(b) Philles Hinde of London. Merchant.
(c) Marriland (?). To serve as a Cordwayner. Hound. Capt. Philles Hinde.
(d) 4th. September 1684. (Abra. Bayly.)

Note :—The last two indentures are very dirty and damaged.

This list contains all the Indentures which have survived. Some of the names are very difficult to read, being a mere scrawl. In many cases where a signature of the Apprentice appears, it would seem to have been written by some-one else. If any reader finds an entry of interest, it should be checked with the original to make sure that it is correct. The names of Towns and Counties are probably spelt according to local pronunciation and are difficult to identify.

Early Emigrants to America from Liverpool

The following valuable list of early emigrants to America has been sent to us by Mr. R. Sharpe France, County Archivist for Lancashire. The original manuscript is in the Lancashire Record Office, County Hall, Preston.

QSP 625/2 1686

Quarter Sessions

The names of such persons who voluntarilie came before Oliver Lyme Esquire Maior of Leverpoole, and were examined and bound by Indentures under their hands and seales to serve the severall persons undernamed or their assignes, the terme of foure yeares after their arrivall in Virginia or Mariland in America.

1686	Servants to Gilbert Livesley of Leverpoole marriner
10th June	Hugh Owen of Wrexham in the Countie of Denbigh laborer aged 24 yeares
12th June	Elizabeth Jones of the Cittie of Westchester spinster aged 21 yeares
19th June	John Joanes of Wrexham in the Countie of Denbigh laborer aged 21 yeares
29th June	George Walker of Astburie in the Countie of Chester blacksmith aged 27 yeares
ditto	Ann Cooper of Lydiate in the Countie of Lancaster spinster aged 21 yeares
7 Julye	William Evans of the Cittie of Bristol llaborer aged 24 yeares
13 Julye	Alice Jenkinson of Warrington in the Countie of Lancaster spinster aged 21 yeares
	Servants to James Hornbye of Leverpoole marriner
29th Julye	Phillis Ferne of Blurton in the Countie of Stafford spinster aged 21 yeares
	Roger Browne of Llandlehide in Carnarvanshire single person aged 21 yeares
13th August	Ann Johnson of Kinsley in the Countie of Chester spinster aged 21 yeares
	Servants to Edward Tarleton of Leverpoole marriner
6th August	Joan Norres of the Isle of Man spinster aged 26 yeares

6th August	Alice Lacie of the Isle of Man spinster aged 21 yeares
2nd October	Theophilus Basnett of Kelsall in the Countie of Chester single person aged 22 yeares
ditto	Richard Thomas of Clanriott in the Countie of Denbigh butcher aged 30 yeares

Servants to Thomas Sandiford Junior of Leverpoole merchant

1st September	Joseph Low of Ashton in Mackerfeild laborer aged 22 yeares
10th September	Margrett Thomas of Whitchurch in the Countie of Salopp spinster aged 23 yeares
13th September	Thomas Jones of Northopp in the countie of Flint, milner, aged 22 yeares
ditto	Sarah Barber of Tamworth in the Countie of Stafford spinster aged 22 yeares

Servants to Edmund Croston of Leverpoole marriner

23rd September	William Alsea of Farnham in Hampshire painter aged 22 yeares
ditto	Samuell Chapman of Brundsley in Derbishire taylor aged 21 yeares
ditto	John Richardson of Mansfeild in Nottinghamshire bricklaier aged 22 yeares
ditto	John Gerrard of Parr in the Countie of Lancaster blacksmith aged 30 yeares
ditto	John Shipabottome of Elton neere Burye in Lancashire husbandman aged 27 yeares
ditto	Samuell Sedwell of Manchester in Lancashire weaver aged 24 yeares
ditto	Amye Pendleton of Manchester aforesaid spinster aged 26 yeares
6 October	Joseph Howard of Broadston in Derbishire joyner aged 36 yeares

Servants to John Banckes of Leverpoole marriner

19th August	Isabell Wilkinson of the Cittie of Carlile spinster aged 22 yeares
10th September	Alice Turner of Goosner in Lancashire widdow aged 30 yeares

Servants to Richard Radcliffe of Leverpoole merchant

27th September	John Naylor sonne of Thomas Naylor of Bowas in the Countie of Stafford aged 28 yeares

Servants to Richard Houghton of Leverpoole merchant

6th October John Walker of Belfast in the Kingdome of Ireland merchant aged 19 yeares

Judeth Wiresdell of Woolverhampton in Staffordshire widdow aged 19 yeares

INDEX

APPRENTICES

A
Abell, Robert, 571
Abie (or Obie), George, 271
Adamson, David (Scot), 766
Adamson, George, 283
Agar, Henry, 501
Agersall, Thomas, 758
Alligin, William, 892
Allyn, Luke, 706
Almond, James, 770
Amis, Abraham, 773
Andrew, John, 797
Arden, Susan, 886
Armstrong, John, 967
Arnold, Jeremy, 694
Arundall, Daniel, 472
Ash, Margrett, 996
Ashley, Andrew, 485
Askin, Michael, 439
Ast, John, 511
Atkins, Hannah, 398
Atkinson, Frances, 932
Ayles, Marmaduke, 22

B
Backwell, James, 753
Badger, Jeffery, 686
Bagott, William, 811
Baker, John, 979
Ball, John, 922
Baly, John, 854
Bancks, An, 971
Banister, Francis, 740
Bankes, James, 703
Banton, Joseph, 972
Barker, Francis, 911
Barlow, Thomas, 37
Barnes, Ellinore, 944
Barnes, Nicholas, 612
Barratt, Thomas, 27
Barratt, Thomas, 57
Barrow, Ralf, 726
Barrownouch, Jacob, a Polander, 884
Barton, Martha, 455
Batrum, Abell, 491
Bauldwin, Frances, 890
Baystow, Richard, 677
Beard, Godfrey, 56
Beatson, Susannah, 324
Beckett, John, 741
Beddoe, John, 503
Beman, Elizabeth, 795
Benerley, John, 54
Bennett, John, 310
Bennett, Mary, 903
Betham, Richard, 420
Bettaly, Robert, 52
Betts, Joseph, 381
Bever, Elizabeth, 624
Bignall, Rebecca, 273
Billing, John, 907
Bings, William, 978
Bird, Elizabeth, 832
Bird, John, 566
Bisford, Henry, 784
Blake, Henry, 62
Boddard, Henry, 468
Bond, John, 693
Boreman, Joseph, 696
Borrodon, Robert, 71
Bower, James, 900
Bowles, John, 379
Bowton, Hannah, 732
Boyer, Robert, 269
Boytor, John, 710
Brace, George, 509
Bradford, John, 23
Braisnett, William, 772
Bramley, Thomas, 47
Bray, Richard, 951
Breeding, Andres (Scot), 809
Brigdon, Thomas, 898
Brisco, Henry, 916
Brittland, John, 477
Bromfield, Francis, 785
Brooks, John, 912
Brown, Ann, 301
Browne, John, 756
Browne, John, 823
Browne, Joshua, 579
Browne, Nicholas, 761
Browne, Richard, 51
Bryant, George, 577
Buck, Obediah, 558
Bullock, Edmond, 46
Bullock, John, 837
Bummer, Thomas, 835
Burnley, Mary, 499
Burton, Thomas, 527
Busby, Mary, 860
Button, Edward, 787

C
Campion, Cornelius, 585
Cannaby? William, 648
Carpenter, William, 980
Carter, Sarah, 623
Cary, Thomas, 900
Cattbury, Thomas, 442
Chambers, Henry, 819
Champly, Samuel, 843
Chapman, Richard, 87
Cheeseman, Robert, 72
Child, Ursula, 692
Chiswell, Mary, 303
Church, Charles, 994
Church, Daniel, 559
Churchill, Jone, 440
Clapp, John, 489
Clapshoe, Robert, 643
Clark, Frances, 861
Clark, Susan, 660
Clark, Susan, 808
Clarkson, Timothy, 662
Claye, Lawrance, 272
Clayton, Edward, 942
Clifford, John, 12
Coaks, Lydea, 441
Cobham, Walter, 364
Cock, Nicholas, 935
Coffin, Francis, 970
Coleman, Francis, 470
Coles, Richard, 653
Collins, John, 902
Colpis, John, 502
Cook, John, 21
Cooper, Benjamin, 452
Cooper, Robert, 433
Copis (or Colpis), John, 502
Cornelis, Pauls (from Holland), 750
Correy, Thomas, 908
Crackwell, John, 938
Crampton, Thomas, 565
Crocker, Richard, 20
Crode, Abell, 775
Croffts, John, 850
Croft, John, 41
Cros, Robert, 708

Croson, George, 685
Croswell, Roger, 321
Cruse, John, 652
Curren, John, 842
Curtis, John, 877

D

Dalby, Thomas, 666
Danby, Edward, 974
Darling, John, 1000
Darnel, Thomas, 857
Darrant, Frances, 899
Davis, Henery, 24
Davis, James, 621
Davis, William, 414
Davison, Peter (Scot), 931
Desper, Christopher, 807
Despur, Lamboth, 26
Dibdon, Kabell, 419
Diggery, Jone, 72
Diptale, Anne, 973
Dixon, Humphrey, 464
Dorson, Rebecca, 284
Dowly, Ann, 640
Downes, William, 809
Dowson, John, 282
Draper, Ellinor, 691
Drummer, Michael, 858
Drummer, Michel, 754
Duckett, Alice, 535
Dunbarr, John (Scot), 656
Dunkley, Thomas, 965
Dwaite, Mary, 828
Dycer, Phillip, of Flushing, 894
Dyer, Thomas, 528
Dyer, William, 736
Dymond, Thomas, 573

E

East, John, 396
Easton, Nicholas, 386
Eaststopp, Richard, 696
Eavfens, Thomas, 737
Edgar, Richard, 869
Edmons, William, 895
Edwards, James, 432
Edwards, John, 70
Elderkin, John, 591
Elkins, Richard, 328
Elletts, Richard, 862
Ellitt, James, 375
Ely, Gabriel, 801
English, Walter, 958
Esmond, Edward, 833
Ethewe, Rachel, 434
Evans, Evan, 389

Evans, Mary, 904
Evans, William, 674
Evered? John, 447
Everill, Seth, 870
Everygen, George, 280

F

Fairbank, John, 40
Falconer, Deborah, 873
Farratt, William, 822
Farrow, Francis, 383
Feaser, William (Scot), 814
Feild, Barbara, 462
Fenwick, William, 998
Fidler, William, 632
Finch, Martin, 32
Fisher, William, 369
Fitch, John, 825
Flack, Henry, 494
Flack, Mary, 536
Fletcher, Elizabeth, 3
Floyd, John, 946
Foller, Thomas, 562
Ford, John, 539
Ford, William, 605
Foredom, William, 388
Fowler, Thomas, 987
Frame, Thomas, 769
Francis, Daniel, 659
Francis, Jacob, a Dutchman, 893
Francklin, Frances, 330
Freeman, Mary, 322
Freman, William, 701
Frost, William, 752

G

Gaint, Charles, 14
Gardner, Alice, 777
Gardner, Daniel, 776
Gardner, Katherine, 826
Gardner, Martin, 782
Geay, Peter, 913
Gent, Samuel, 765
George, Joseph, 749
German, John, 950
Getchell, John, 611
Gibbs, Mary, 681
Gilbert, Mary, 876
Giles, William, 465
Gilmore, John, 337
Glover, Mary, 456
Goldsmith, Mary, 847
Gooding, James, 281
Goodrick, Bozoun, 963
Goreham, Francis, 312
Goring, Gilbert (gent), 31

Gray, James, 484
Gray, Zachariah, 521
Graygoose, Christopher, 5
Green, Sarah, 305
Greene, Mathew, 385
Greene, Thomas, 327
Greene, William, 512
Greenlees, Thomas, 490
Greenwood, John, 883
Gregory, Addam, 603
Gresham, James, 620
Grey, Elizabeth, 976
Griggs, John, 649
Grindy, Thomas, 945
Gurlin, William, 855
Gutterick, Dorothy, 316
Guy, Charles, 438

H

Habbergam, James, 43
Haddock, Giles, 515
Hadely, John, or Hadley, 927
Haines, Thomas, 689
Haires, Francis, 614
Hall, John, 631
Hall, John, 992
Hall or Hawe, John, 954
Hambledon, Anthony, 318
Hancock, Arthur, 993
Hanly, William, 896
Hannam, John, 331
Hannam, John, 570
Hanworth, Elizabeth, 658
Harbridge, Henry, 443
Hardin, William, 641
Harding, Cathrine, 939
Harding, John, 794
Hargoose, Stephen, 355
Harrex, William, 622
Harris, Elizabeth, 790
Harris, Frederick, 999
Harris, John, 679
Harris, Mary, 307
Harris, Mary, 880
Harris, Richard, 4
Harris, William, 646
Harrison, Robert, 836
Harrison, Thomas, 42
Harrison, William, 786
Harrison, William, 827
Harvey, Elizabeth, 315
Harvey, Joyce, 852
Harwood, John, 294
Hasteed, William, 731
Haster, John, 821

Hastings, Mary, 923
Haveland, William, 4
Hawes, Amy, 663
Hawkins, John, 39
Haye (?Hope), William, 530
Hearne, Thomas, 995
Heather, Edward, 504
Hellmore, Trustram, 13
Hennagin, John, 469
Henry, John, 436
Hepart, Richard, 63
Herick, Thomas, 557
Hern, Thomas, or Hearne, 995
Herne, George, 738
Hewit, Mary, 711
Heyward, Thomas, 540
Hicks, Richard, 606
Hide, Phillipp, 639
Hiland or Hyland, James, 949
Hildridge, Frances, 933
Hill, An, 783
Hill, John, 744
Hill, Rebecca, 789
Hill, Robert, 416
Hillard, Richard, 905
Hilton, Sarah, 389
Hinde, Richard, 302
Hippy, William, 563
Holland, Thomas, 9
Hollis, John, 779
Holmes, John, 279
Holmes, Richard, 982
Holmes, William, 588
Holt, Edward, 638
Holt, Richard, 526
Holtham, Thomas, 682
Honeywell, Thomas, 479
Honywell, Joseph, 940
Hooper, Walter, 581
Hope, William, 530
Horne, John, 445
Horsey, Ralfe, 730
Horton, Charles, 792
Horton, John, 804
Horton, William, 872
Howard, Lawrence, 713
Howarth, Thomas, 568
Howes, Richard, 739
Howlett, William, 371
Hudson, Edmund, 947
Humphreys, Richard, 618
Hutchins, Mary, 742
Hutchinson, Dorothy, 522
Hutton, An, 984

Hutton, Susan, 985
Hutton, Thomas, 669
Hyland, James, 949

I

Igne, John, 668
Ingram, Henry, 705
Ivory, Elizabeth, 546
Ivory, George, 415

J

Jackson, Elizabeth, 319
Jackson, Richard, 38
Jackson, Savile, 610
Jackson, William, 887
Jenkins, Mary, 457
Jenkins, Mary, 661
Jennings, Dorothy, 687
Johnson, Elizabeth, 636
Johnson, James, 372
Johnson, John, 673
Johnson, John, 816
Johnson, Joseph, 627
Johnson, Peter, 463
Johnson, Robert, 909
Johnson, Samuel, 473
Johnson, Thomas, 629
Jones, Elizabeth, 707
Jones, Howell, 288
Jones, Hugh, 981
Jones, Humphry, 748
Jones, James, 372
Jones, Joel, 59
Jones, Margaret (Irish), 534
Jones, Richard, 437

K

Kelton, Thomas, 467
Kett, Benjamin, 937
Key, George, 675
Key, William, 392
Kible, Hannah, 645
Kilmore, Richard, 578
Kilner, Richard, or Kilmore, 578
Kimber, Martha, 311
Kimberley, Thomas, 655
Kimpson, James, 517
King, George, 50
King, George, 897
King, John, 510
Kinsbury, John, 431
Krim (or Kym), John, 471
Kym, John, 471
Kynner, Thomas, 934

L

Lake, Aaron, 67
Lanford, Thomas, 626
Langston, Mary, 863
Lankford, Thomas, or Lanford, 626
Laurence? George, 957
Law, John (Scot), 604
Lawton, Elizabeth, 917
Laymard, John (French), 49
Leatherington, Nicholas, 68
Lee, Henry, 735
Lee, John, 796
Lee, Joseph, 830
Lee, Samuel, 829
Leek (or Lake), Aaron, 67
Leeson, Symon, 590
Lefeadero, Sarah (Dutch), 977
Lestrange, Thomas, 584
Levens, Benjamin, 514
Lewis, David, 381
Lewis, Jeane, 290
Lewis, Thomas, 635
Lingwood, Thomas, 793
Liptrapp? Elizabeth! 688
Lithemore, William, 831
Little, Robert, or Littler, 806
Lodge, Thomas, 561
Lolley, Thomas, 910
Lomax, John, 450
Lowdon, John, 613
Lucas, Thomas, 813
Luke, Thomas, 888
Lyle, William, 941
Lynes, Elizabeth, 642

M

Macherness, Edward, 743
Macquin, Daniel, 762
Maginn, Daniel, or Macquin, 762
Malin, John, 323
Manning, Abigail, 885
Maple, Benjamin, 550
Marchbanck, Elinor, 704
Markley, James (French), 928
Marsh, Joseph, 6
Marshall, Joseph, 304
Martin, Humphry, 518
Martin, Thomas, 820
Mason, Elizabeth, 277

Mason, George, 508
Mastys, Margaret, 278
Mather, John, 616
Mathews, Thomas, 955
Mattson, Andrew, 746
May, Mary, 763
Mayhoe, William, 30
Mayne, Nathaniel, 601
Meade, William, 395
Mercer, Elizabeth, 924
Mercer, Robert, 788
Merring, Elizabeth, 607
Midleton, Joseph, 476
Miles, Hannah, 394
Miller, Jonathan, 771
Mitchell, John, 297
Mitchell, Mary, 721
Moody, John, 802
Morall, John, 630
Morerie, John, 8
Morrell, John, 919
Morres, William, 376
Morrey, Sarah, 650
Morris, Jacob, 943
Morton, Christopher, 446
Morton, Mathew, 654
Morton, Robert, 444
Mullinex, Richard, 865

N

Nason, Thomas, 291
Naylor, John, 986
Naylor, Thomas, 745
Nelsom, Edward, 920
Nibbs, Richard, 552
Nightsmith, Thomas, 295
Norcolt, Richard, 845
Norman, Samuel, 478
Northerow, Samuel, 292

O

Obie, George, 271
Ogden, Abraham, 882
Oglevie, David (Scot), 846
Oswald, Andrew, 634
Owene, John, 529
Owin, Hugh, 270
Owines, Thomas, 286

P

Pagrame? Joseph, 547
Paice, Jacob, 507
Paine, Thomas, 482
Palmer, Nathanell, 969
Palmer, Oliver, 889
Parker, Sarah, 960
Parkington, Hugh, 487

Parsons, George, 551
Passmore, John, 555
Peachie, John, 18
Peacock, Richard, 867
Peal, Robert, 637
Pearce, Francis, 549
Pearson, William, 582
Peatey, Richard, 595
Peckden, Williams, 716
Peirson, Mary, 296
Peisley? Robert, 378
Pelham, Mary, 997
Pepper, Ursilla, 202
Perry, Susannah, 727
Peters, Thomas, 285
Pettenreck? Robert (Scot), 767
Pettie, Richard, 486
Pewtow? John, 966
Phelix, Henry, 757
Phillips, Benjamin, 780
Phillips, Edward, 667
Phillips, Sarah, 597
Phillips, William, 351
Phillips, William, 520
Piddock, Elizabeth, 803
Pike, Lidea, 841
Pilkington, Margret, 724
Pingler? William, 351
Pirkins, John, 817
Pooke, Simon, 314
Poole, Francis, 556
Porter, Benjamin, 548
Porter, John, 592
Powell, Edward, 513
Powell, Elizabeth, 715
Powell, Nathaniel, 44
Prentice, William, 553
Preston, George, 538
Price, Anne, 733
Price, Evan, 799
Price, George or Gregory, 560
Price? Hugh, 657
Price, Richard, 760
Price, Samuel, 16
Prichard, Everilday, 300
Prince, John, 28
Prou, Cyprian, 952
Prou? Margaret, 951

R

Rachell, John, 572
Ratcliffe, Samuel, 596
Rawlett, Dockas, 805
Rawlings, John, 516
Reader, Martha, 293

Reed, John (Scot), 768
Reeve, John, 929
Rest, Moses, 959
Reynelds, Richard, 576
Reynolds, Robert, 10
Rice, John, 498
Rice, Edmund, 380
Richardson, Samuel, 275
Richerson, Mary, 975
Ricky, Abraham, 483
Riggs, James, 699
Rissie? Mary, 496
Robinson, John, 853
Robinson, John, 956
Robson, John, 956
Roger, William, 915
Rogers, John, 53
Rogers, John and Hester 435
Rogers, Margaret, 276
Rook, George, 617
Rose, Benjamin, 859
Rose, Richard, 906
Rowland, Thomas, 542
Rowlson, Nicholas, 460
Ruffs, Jacob, 35
Ryall, Phillipp, 326

S

Saly, Mary, 594
Sanders, William, 664
Sandyford, Mary, 17
Sasfield, Patrick, 537
Savage, Thomas, 608
Scarr, William, 569
Sclater, Thomas, 583
Scott, Mathew, 747
Scott, Robert, 651
Seafield, Robert, 670
Searl, Sarah, 719
Seddich, John, 481
Seethings, John, 575
Selnister, Elizabeth, 384
Sergiant, Lewis, 15
Serne, Charles, 19
Setre, Michell, or Micah, 34
Shafield, Isaac, 342
Sharp, Nicholas, 676
Sharp, Thomas, 69
Shelton, John, 812
Shephard, Grace, 274
Shipperson, Anne, 449
Simons, William, 480
Sison, Thomas, or Sisson, 308
Siviter, Charles, 878

Skinner, John, 988
Skipp, Elizabeth, 567
Smale, Zacheriah, 299
Smart, John, 702
Smeethes, Thomas, 598
Smith, Jane, 864
Smith, John, 298
Smith, John, 448
Smith, John, 532
Smith, John, 764
Smith, Thomas (Irish), 58
Smith, Thomas, 474
Smyth, Nicholas, 936
Sneath, Hugh, 541
Snell, Richard, 11
Snellgrove, Henry, 615
Solley, John, 531
Sparkes, Joseph, 524
Speakman, Frances, 695
Spencer, Mary, 600
Spurling, Richard, 488
Stafford, Richard, 364
Standley, William, 647
Stansell, John, 387
Stanton, John, 838
Stanton, Mary, 962
Start, John, 329
Steele, Isaac, 391
Steele, Robert, 377
Steere, Abel, 55
Steevens, Robert, 968
Stennet, John, or Stennitt, 856
Stevenes, Thomas, 397
Stevens, Alice, 918
Stoell, Bartholomew, 628
Stokely, John, 961
Stott, Francis, 791
Stratford, Anthony, 672
Street, William, 500
Strowd, William, 871
Surey, Henry, 289
Sutheth, Henry, 325
Swain, James, 543
Swaisland, Richard, 948
Swann, Richard, 874
Swann, Thomas, 475
Swanson, Matthew, 891
Symmer, William, 29
Symmons, Jacob, 45
Symmons (or Simons), William, 480

T

Taggwell, William, 665
Talbott, Edward, 733
Tasker, Robert, 554
Taubutt, Elizabeth, 495
Taylor, Abigall, 306
Taylor, Abraham, 781
Taylor, Edward, 337
Taylor, Edward, 881
Tempest, Arabella, 844
Terrold, George, 714
Thomas, William, 451
Thompson, John, 602
Thompson, Katherine, 390
Thompson, William, 587
Thomson, William, 564
Thomson, William, 751
Thorpe, James, 544
Tomkin, John, 953
Towell, Charles, 497
Towne, John, 599
Townsend, William, 875
Trelford, Richard, 609
Troke, Sarah, 644
Trope, George, 755
Truell, John, 453
Trunkett, Jane, 926
Tubb, John, 66
Tyler, John, 60
Tynn, Mabel, 728

U

Underwood, Henry, 466

V

Vaughan, Joseph, 774

W

Wakefield, Thomas, 671
Walker, Thomas, 718
Wallis, John, 5
Walters, Thomas, 36
Ward, Edmond, 729
Ward, Jonathan, 680
Ward, William, 678
Wardle, Francis, 574
Watts, Elizabeth, 709
Watts, Marke, 815
Weaver, Mary, 320
Webb, Charles, 7
Webb, Charles, 33
Webb, Elizabeth, 989
Webb, Hannah, 798
Webster, Thomas, 25
Weldon, Thomas, 734
Weller, Margaret, 625
Wells, Dinah, 683
Wendright, William, 834
Weston, Robert, 519
Wetton, John, 61
Whaley, William, 417
Wharton, Susan, 721
Whitby, Robert, 983
White, John, 580
White, Richard, 759
White, Robert, 493
Whitehead, John, or Whiting, 586
Whitfield, Jane, 533
Whiting, John, 586
Whiting, William, 525
Whiting, William, 589
Wigelsworth, Ambros, 866
Wilkinson, Elizabeth, 523
Williams, David, 921
Williams, Davie, 991
Williams, Elizabeth, 712
Williams, John, 505
Williams, Luke, 848
Williams, Robert, 700
Williams, Stephen, 778
Williams, Thomas, 717
Williams, Thomas, 964
Williamson, John, 315
Willis, Henry, 684
Willoby, Theophilus, 374
Wilsheire, William, 48
Wilson, Henry, 506
Wilson, Henry, 541
Wilson, John, 458
Wilson, Joseph, 418
Wilson, Symon, 824
Winch, John, 720
Winter, Charles, 925
Withers, William, 461
Wood, Henry, 690
Wood, James, 930
Wood, John, 721
Wood, Mary, 697
Wooton, Thomas, 393
Worrell, Richard, 800
Wrangham, George, 492
Wright, John, 619
Wright, Robert, 633
Wright, Stephen, 849
Wright, Walter, 990
Wrinch, Mary, 309

Y

York, Thomas, 593
Young, Jone, 454

INDEX

PERSONS TO WHOM APPRENTICES WERE BOUND

A
Acres, Jacob (Mar), 841
Adams, Robert (Jamaica), 450
Adams, Robert and Ann, 415
Arche, Robert (Mer), 716

B
Ball, Joseph (Capt), 8
Ballard, William (Mar), 939
Bancks, John, 305
Batt, Richard (Gent), 513
Batts, Richard (Mer), 278
Bayly, Richard (Mar), of Maryland, 618
Becker, John, 320
Beeding, William (Mar), 582
Bennett, John (Mer), 389
Berrisford, Thomas (Mer), 922
Berry, Samuel (Surg), 958
Bills, Richard (Mar), 202
Blacke, Francis, 72
Boile, Thomas (Surg), of Jamaica, 462
Bowman, John (Mer), 989
Bradshaw, Thomas (Mar), 704
Branson, Francis, 34
Bray, Richard, 913
Brayner, James (Mer), 600
Bright, John (Mer), 566.
Brook, Edward, 274
Brooks, Edward (Mer), 995
Brown, John (Capt), 632
Browne, John (Mer), 561
Browne, Peregrine, 626
Bull, Joseph (Mar), 364
Burford, Edward, of Virginia, 674

C
Car, David, (Mar), or Carr, 812
Carey, Thomas (Mar), 324
Carr, David (Mar), 562
Carter, John (Mer), 941
Chamberlain, Thomas (Mar), 723
Clapham, Daniel (Mar), 855
Clark, Abraham, of Maryland, 878
Clarke, John (Mer), 337
Cocking, Thomas, 715
Collington, Peter, Kt, 482
Congden, James, 307
Coning, Richard (Mar), 503
Connaway, James (Mar), 292
Corbett, Edward (Mar), 683

D
Daniel, Christopher (Mar), 726
Day, John (Mer), 999
Deane, Christopher (Mer), 371
Dicks, John, 631
Dix, John (Mer), 504
Dodson, John, (Mer), 834
Dowkera, William (Mer), 453
Dunn, Joseph (Mer), 273
Doyne, Thomas (Mar), 479

E
Earl, John (Mar), 758
Edwards, John (Mer), Maryland, 315
Emmerson, James (Mar), 376
Evans, Luis, of Maryland, Planter, 844
Everard, Thomas (Mar), 827
Evilling, Christopher (Mar), 297

F
Fles, Thomas (Mar), 327
Frare, Tobias (mer), 418
French, Francis (Mer), 830
Frisby, William (Mer), Maryland, 889
Fulborne, Moses (Mar), 925

G
Gadsden, Thomas (Mer), 991
Gallaway, James (Mar), 795
Galwith, James, 322
Galwith, John, Maryland, 325
Garbrane, Harke (Mer), 530
George, William, 508
Goodburn, William (Mer), 506
Gower, Phillipp, 398
Green, George (Mar), 700
Green, Thomas, 337
Greene, Peter, 895
Grubb, Thomas (Mar), 891

H
Hall, John (Mer), 527
Hall, Robert (Mar), 682
Harton, Robert (Mar), 845
Haslewood, John (Mer), 650
Hatch, Walter (Mer), 271
Haveland, William (Mer), 9
Heyward, Daniel (Mar), 607
Hide, Phineas (Capt), 664
Hill, John (Mer), 537
Howeland, William (Mer), 378

Humphries, John (Mar), 522
Hutchens, William (Mer), 613

J

Jackson, John, 290
James, John (Mer), 678
Jefcole? John (Mar), 863
Johnson, Frederick (Mar), 742
Johnson, Henry, Kt (Mer), 603
Johnson, William (Mar), 269
Jones, John (Mer), 512
Jordain, Thomas (Mar), 841

K

Keckerbatt, Arnatt, 319

L

Leach, John (Mar), 33
Lee, Francis (Mer), 377
Lee, John (Mer), 281
Leech, Jonas (Capt), 9
Lehunt, George (Mer), 535
Lessells, John (Mar), 61
Lockton, Robert (Mar), 802
Longman, James (Mar), 668
Lucey, Richard, 296
Lyon, Isaac (Mar), 642

M

May, John (Mer), 608
Molborn, Richard (Mar), 857
Moore, James (Mer), 572
More, John (Mer), 955
Morley, Thomas, Planter, of Barbados, 866
Mosse, Richard (Mar), 641
Murphy, Richard (Mer), 275

N

Nash, Samuel (Mer), 7
Neale, John (Mer), 515
Newbold, Thomas (Mer), 872
Norris, John (Mer), 516

O

Oates, Bartholomew (Mar), 890
Orton, William (Mar), 546

P

Padly, Edward (Mar), 778
Pain, Edmond (Mer), 548
Pain, Francis (Mar), 414
Paine, Edmund (Mar), 520
Paine, Joseph, 460
Painter, Nicholas (Mer), 986
Painter, Nicholas, of Maryland, Gent, 949

Pamle, Nicholas, of Maryland, Gent, 943
Parles, Charles, 316
Parsons, Francis (Mar), 457
Parties, Francis (Mer), 619
Patterson, Edward, 3
Pattman, Edmund (Mer), 771
Peak, Pater (Mar), 593
Pearson, John (Mer), 571
Peggin, Peter (Mer), 640
Perce, John (Mar), 638
Peterson, Andrew (Mar), 743
Pewsey, Williams, 792
Philip, James (Mar), 790
Phillips, James, 286
Phillips, Samuel, 289
Phillips, William (Mar), 435
Potter, John (Mar), 697
Prin, Nicholas (Mar), 304
Prince, Mathew, 390
Prissitt, Christopher (Mar), 483
Prym, Nicholas (Mar), 461
Purifoy, Michael (Mar), 318
Purvis, John (Mar), 384
Putman, Edmund (Mer), 833

R

Randall, John (Esq), 432
Rennet, John (Mar), 464
Richardson, Francis, 48
Richardson, Thomas (Surg), 533
Rider, Mathew (Mar), 391
Robinson, Maximilian (Mer), 936
Rowe, John (Mer), 517
Russell, Robert (Mar), 420

S

Sanders, John (Mer), 508
Sandiford, Edmond, of Barbados, Planter, 693
Shawe, John (Mer), 511
Sloper, Thomas, Maryland, 454
Smith, George (Mer), 542
Smith, John (Mer), 381
Smyth, Nicholas (Mar), 624
Smyth, William, 26
Snelling, Peter, 868
Snow, Nathaniel, 306
Somes, William (Mer), 574
Staples, Michael (Mar), 871
Stoder, Samson, 763
Stone, John (Mer), 524
Stubbs, Thomas (Mer), 543
Sweet, Thomas (Mar), 597

T

Talbott, Edward (Mer), 630
Tannor, John (Mar), 992

Tench, Thomas (Mer), 699
Thorne, John, 301
Tragany, Henry (Mer), 565
Trynion, Matthew (Mar), 463
Turpin, John (Mar), 580
Twilt, John (Mar), 899
Twitt, John (Mar), 706

W

Wallinger, Anthony (Mer), 416
Ward, Thomas, of Jamaica, Planter, 63
Waterhouse, Randsford (Mer), 605
Waterhouse, Richard (Mer), 521
Watts, Bartholomew (Mar), 877
Webb, William, Virginia, 451
Whaley, James (Mer), 622
White, John, 69
White, Samuel, 300
Wild, Abraham (Mer), 900
Wilkey, John (Mer), 624
Williams, James (Mer), 509
Williams, John (Mer), 419
Williams, Samuel (Mar), 924
Wilson, John, 276
Wise, Thomas (Mer), 519
Wiseman, John (Mer), 525
Woosley, John, 288
Wosey, Joseph (Mer), 732
Wrayford, William (Mer), 472
Wyche, Thomas (Mer), 299

Y

Yoakley, Michael (Mar), 856
Yorke, William (Mar), 458

CAPTAINS AND SHIPS

Captain	Ship	First Ref.	Country	Sailed
Arnold, Thomas, or Arnall	Jefferies	D.717	Virginia	Sept. 1684
Ball, Joseph	Hopewell	B.10	Barbados	Mar. 1683
Bartholomew,	Providence	B.515	Jamaica	May 1684
Bedding, William	Friendship	B.545	Barbados	Jan. 1684
Bennett, John	William	B.389	Jamaica	Nov. 1683
Bird, Daniel	Charles	B.385	Virginia	Nov. 1683
Bond, Giles	William & Robert	B.416	Barbados	Feb. 1684
Bowman,		D.622	Antigua	July 1684
Brakes, John	Joseph	B.760	Jamaica	Apr. 1684
Bridgman,	George	B.514	Nevis & Jamaica	Mar. 1684
Bridgman, Richard, or Brigham	Francis & Dorothy	B.519	Antigua	Mar. 1684
Burford, Edward	Abraham & Francis	D.643	Maryland	Aug. 1684
Carey, Thomas	Adventure	D.433	Maryland	Nov. 1683
Connaway, James	Baltimore	B.292	Maryland	Sept. 1683
Cooper, Ralph	Adventure	B.630	Maryland	July 1684
Croft, Thomas	Crowne	B.506	Barbados	Apr. 1684
Dunn, Thomas	St George	B.472	Nevis	Dec. 1683
Emberley,	Katherine	B.573	Barbados	Mar. 1684
Evilling, Christopher	William & Thomas	B.297	Virginia	Sept. 1683
Guester	Hanna	B.281	Maryland	Sept. 1683
Harris, John	Mary	B.270	Maryland	Nov. 1683
Harvey, Isaac	Ann & Mary	B.527	Antigua	May 1684
Hasteed, Thomas, or Hastings	Recoverie	B.299	Carolina	Sept. 1684
Hill, John	Virginia 'Furtop'?	B.381	Virginia	Nov. 1683
Hinde, Philles	Hound	D.982	Maryland	Nov. 1683
Johnson, William	Content	B.269	Maryland	Nov. 1683
Jones,	George	B.525	Jamaica	May 1684
Jones, John	Joseph & Ashton	B.603	Carolina	Apr. 1684
Keazer,	Elizabeth & Katherine	D.695	Maryland	Aug. 1684
Kendall,	Hannah	SF.469	Jamaica	Aug. 1684
Kenzar,	John & Elizabeth	D.684	Maryland	Aug. 1684
Leech, Jonas	John & Elizabeth	B.9	Barbados	Feb. 1683
Longman,	Golden Lyon	D.650	Maryland	Aug. 1684
Mingian, or Mingnon	William & Mary	D.560	Jamaica	Jan. 1684
Norrington, John	Unicorn	B.382	Virginia	Nov. 1684
Pagan, Peter	Booth	D.566	Virginia	July 1864
Parties, Francis	Benedict Leonard	D.623	Maryland	July 1684
Phillips, William	Love	B.435	Maryland	Dec. 1683
Prin or Pryn, Nicholas	Richard & Elizabeth	B.304	Virginia	Sept. 1684
Prissitt, Christopher, or Prissick or Pressick	Barbados Merchant	B.483	Barbados	Mar. 1684

CAPTAINS AND SHIPS (contd.)

Captain	Ship	First Ref.	Country	Sailed
Purvis, John	Duke of Yorke	B.338	Maryland	Nov. 1683
Rogers, Thomas	Loyall Subject	D.698	Maryland	Aug. 1684
Ryder, Matthew	Barnaby	B.371	Virginia	Nov. 1683
Staples, Michael	Crowne Malago	D.666	Maryland	July 1684
Strong, James	Assistance	D.730	Maryland	Sept. 1684
Stubbs, Thomas	Richard & Sarah	B.543	Jamaica	May 1684
Tippitt or Typott,	Mary	B.364	Maryland	Nov. 1683
Tragany, Henry	Brothers Adventure	B.565	Maryland	June 1684
Trim or Tryin,	Judith	B.419	Virginia	Dec. 1683
Wilson, Jonathan	Prince	D.509	Barbados	July 1684

www.ingramcontent.com/pod-product-compliance
Lightning Source LLC
Chambersburg PA
CBHW070509090426
42735CB00012B/2711